FEDERALISM
IMPERATIVE IN POST-CONFLICT AFRICA

**LOOH PRESS THESES SERIES.
VOLUME 3**

FEDERALISM
IMPERATIVE IN POST-CONFLICT AFRICA:
THE CASE OF SOMALIA

GULED SALAH, PhD

1446/2024
Leicester, England
Mogadishu, Somalia

LOOH PRESS LTD.
Copyright © Guled Salah Barre 2024
First Edition, First Print October 2024

All rights reserved.
No part of this publication may be reproduced, stored in any retrieval system, or transmitted in any form or by any means, including photocopying, recording, or other electronic or mechanical methods, without the prior written permission of the publisher, except in the case of brief quotations embodied in critical reviews and certain other non-commercial uses permitted by copyright law.

For permission and requests, write to the publisher or the author, at the address below.

PRINTED & DISTRIBUTED BY
Looh Press Ltd.
56 Lethbridge Close
Leicester, LE1 2EB
England. UK
www.LoohPress.com
LoohPress@gmail.com

CONTACT AUTHOR:
guuleed51@gmail.com

A catalogue record for this book is available from the British Library.
British Library Cataloguing-in-Publication Data

COVER DESIGN & TYPESET
Kusmin (Looh Press)

ISBN
978-1-912411-83-2.   (Hardback)
978-1-912411-84-9.   (Paperback)

CONTENTS

PUBLISHER'S NOTE IX
DEDICATION XI
ACKNOWLEDGMENTS XIII
FOREWORD XV
PREFACE XXIII
INTRODUCTION XXVII

**PART 1. THE EVOLUTION *of* FEDERALISM: HISTORICAL *&*
CONTEMPORARY PERSPECTIVES** 01

**CHAPTER 1. HISTORY *&* CONCEPT *of* FEDERALISM:
A COMPREHENSIVE OVERVIEW** 03
    1.1. Introduction 04
    1.2. Defining ederalism 05
    1.3. Historical Origins and Evolution of Federalism 09
    1.4. Philosophical Basis: Unity and Diversity 14
    1.5. Federalism, Democracy and Politics 15
    1.6. Federalism, Conflict and Peace Settings 18
    1.7. Federalism as Intersystem Governance 20
    1.8. Criticisms and Limitations of Federalism 21
    1.9. The Future of Federalism 23

**CHAPTER 2. COMPARATIVE ANALYSIS OF FEDERALISM:
GLOBAL PERSPECTIVES** 27
    2.1. Introduction 28
    2.2. Federalism in Established Democracies (United States, Canada, Germany) 29
    2.3. Federalism in Multinational States (India, Switzerland, Belgium) 32
    2.4. Federalism in Emerging Economies (Brazil, Nigeria, Russia) 36

2.5. Federalism in Post-Conflict Societies (Bosnia, Herzegovina, Ethiopia, Iraq) 40
　　2.6. Comparative Analysis of Fiscal Federalism 43
　　2.7. Governance and Political Participation in Federal Systems 48
　　2.8. Federalism and Social Policy 50

CHAPTER 3. FEDERALISM IN POST-CONFLICT AFRICAN CONTEXTS: A PATH TO PEACE AND STABILITY 55
　　3.1. Introduction 56
　　3.2. Historical Context of Post-Conflict Situations in Africa 56
　　3.3. Evolution of Federalism in Africa 58
　　3.4. Federalism as a Response to Post-Conflict Challenges . 61
　　3.5. Institutional Design and Implementation of Federal Systems 63
　　3.6. Impact of Federalism on Political Stability and Governance 65
　　3.7. Federalism and Socioeconomic Development 67
　　3.8. Ethno-political Considerations in Federal Structures ... 69
　　3.9. Examining Federalism in Ethiopia, Nigeria, and South Africa 71
　　3.10. Challenges and Criticisms of Federalism in Africa 75
　　3.11. Lessons Learned and Future Prospects 77

PART 2. FEDERALISM IN SOMALIA: CHALLENGES, PROGRESS AND PROSPECTS 81

CHAPTER 4. FOUNDATIONS AND CONTEXTS: HISTORICAL AND CONSTITUTIONAL PERSPECTIVES 83
　　4.1. Introduction 84
　　4.2. Governance in Somalia: A Historical Overview 84
　　4.3. Historical Path of Federalism in Somalia 96
　　4.4. Challenges and Delays in Implementing Federalism in Somalia 100
　　4.5. Islam, Somali Culture, and Federalism: An Integrated Perspective 102

4.6. Federalism and the Provisional Constitution of Somalia 106

CHAPTER 5. FACTORS SHAPING FEDERALISM IN SOMALIA ..119
5.1. Introduction 120
5.2. Overview of the Factors Shaping Federalism 121
5.3. Federalism Deals with Political Division and Mistrust 123
5.4. Weak Institutions and Resource Constraints Hamper Federalism 125
5.5. Peaceful Regions Promote Federalism 129
5.6. Federalism Helps Overcome National Fragmentation 130
5.7. Federalism Accommodates All Parties 131
5.8. The Somali People's Affiliation to Their Regions Favors Federalism 132
5.9. Improved Development in Somali Regions Favors Federalism 133
5.10. Other Factors Observed to Shape Federalism in Somalia 134

CHAPTER 6. TOOLS AND INSTRUMENTS GUIDING FEDERALISM IN SOMALIA 135
6.1. Introduction 136
6.2. General Overview of the Tools and Instruments Guiding Federalism 137
6.3. The Provisional Constitution 139
6.4. Federal Government Laws and Regulations 140
6.5. Intergovernmental Cooperative Frameworks 142
6.6. Laws and Mechanisms for Funds Transfer 144
6.7. Harmonized Monetary and Fiscal Policies 144
6.8. Clear Roles and Responsibilities for the Federal Government and for Member States 146
6.9. Laws and Regulations of Member States 147
6.10. Other Factors That Affect the Tools and Instruments Guiding Federalism in Somalia 148

CHAPTER 7. PUBIC AWARENESS OF FEDERALISM AND ITS DEVELOPMENTAL IMPACT 149
    7.1.   Introduction 150
    7.2.   Awareness of the Preferred Governance System 150
    7.3.   Awareness of Power-Sharing Arrangements 152
    7.4.   Federalism's Impact on Political Development 155
    7.5.   Federalism's Impact on Social and Economic Development 157

CHAPTER 8. WEAKNESSES OF FEDERALISM IN SOMALIA & REQUIRED REFORMS 161
    8.1.   Introduction 162
    8.2.   General Overview of the Weaknesses of Federalism in Somalia 162
    8.3.   Lack of a Clear Definition of the Type of Federalism Practiced in Somalia 164
    8.4.   Lack of an Effective Mechanism to Resolve Disputes. 165
    8.5.   Lack of Capacity and Resources for the Federal Government 166
    8.6.   Lack of Agreement on Key Issues during Establishment of the Federal System 166
    8.7.   Lack of Coordination between the Federal Government and Member States 167
    8.8.   Required Reforms 168

CHAPTER 9. CONCLUSION AND PROPOSED FRAMEWORK . 173
    9.1.   Introduction 174
    9.2.   Summary of Analysis 176
    9.3.   Proposed Framework 191
REFERENCES 207
INDEX 221

PUBLISHER'S NOTE

ABOUT LOOH PRESS THESES SERIES

The "*Looh Press Theses Series*" aims to bring to our readers some of the rare and unpublished theses available in Somali, Arabic and English. Some of these theses are unique, others are impactful but have never been published. For the purpose of accessibility to specialists and non-specialists alike, some of these theses are published as they are, with minor editorial efforts, whilst others are completely rewritten, with new introductions. Some are abridged for the purpose of wider readership. As such, the series aims to enrich the library of Somali studies and provide a valuable resource for scholars and general readers alike.

The series stands as a pioneering initiative in academic publishing, dedicated to bringing exceptional doctoral research in social studies to the forefront of scholarly discourse.

The Looh Press Theses Series is its commitment to making valuable scholarly work accessible to a broader audience. Many exceptional theses remain confined within university repositories or exist only as unpublished manuscripts. By transforming these works into published volumes, we ensure that crucial research findings reach the wider academic community and inform policy discussions, especially in the area of Social Studies.

The series primarily focuses on social studies relating to Somalia and the Horn of Africa, addressing critical gaps in the literature. However, we also welcome comparative studies that place regional dynamics within global contexts, ensuring our publications contribute to broader theoretical discussions in social sciences.

FEDERALISM IMPERATIVE IN POST-CONFLICT AFRICA: THE CASE OF SOMALIA

We are proud to present "Federalism Imperative in Post-Conflict Africa: The Case of Somalia" by Dr Guled Salah Barre, a groundbreaking contribution to our understanding of federal governance in post-conflict societies. This exceptional work is enriched by insightful forewords from two distinguished scholars: Dr Abdiwali Gas, whose expertise in political economy and governance has influenced policy across the Horn of Africa, and Prof Abdurahman Badiyow, a renowned authority on Islamic studies and Somali politics.

This thesis represents a paradigm shift in how we conceptualise federalism in post-conflict African contexts. Dr Barre's comprehensive analysis spans historical, theoretical and practical dimensions of federalism, offering crucial insights for both academic discourse and policy implementation. The work is particularly timely as Somalia continues its complex journey toward stable federal governance.

As Somalia continues its federal experiment, and as other post-conflict societies consider federal solutions, the insights contained in this volume will prove invaluable for understanding and implementing effective federal governance systems. We are confident that this volume will become a cornerstone reference for scholars and practitioners working on federalism, post-conflict reconstruction and African politics.

Mohammed Abdullah Artan
Founder and Director of Looh Press

DEDICATION

To my beloved mother Asho Ali Mohamoud, the beacon of light in my life's journey. Your unwavering love and guidance have been my greatest source of strength and inspiration. In raising me single-handedly, you have shown me the true meaning of resilience and grace. This book is not just a culmination of my achievements, but a testament to your extraordinary spirit and to the boundless love you have bestowed upon me. You are behind every word, every idea, and every success. Thank you for being my everything.

ACKNOWLEDGMENTS

I extend my deepest gratitude to Almighty Allah for His boundless mercy and guidance, which have been my source of strength and inspiration throughout this endeavor.

My heartfelt appreciation goes to my family, whose unwavering support and love have been the bedrock of my dreams and achievements. Your faith in me has been a beacon of hope and strength.

I am immensely grateful to my PhD supervisors, Professor Danial Ekongwe Awang and Professor Samuel Kale Ewusi, for their invaluable knowledge, patience, and transformative mentorship. I also appreciate the diligent work of the data collection team, whose efforts have been fundamental to this research.

Special thanks to the expert peer reviewers, Dr. Abdiweli M. Ali Gas and Professor Abdurahman A. Baadiyow, whose insightful evaluations have greatly enriched this book. Your critiques and perspectives have been essential in refining my arguments.

I also thank my publisher, for their support and guidance in the publishing process, helping transform my manuscript into a published work.

Finally, I thank everyone who has supported me, directly or indirectly. Your encouragement has been invaluable to this book and my personal and professional growth. Thank you all for being part of this remarkable journey.

FOREWORD

FEDERALISM IN POST-CONFLICT SOMALIA ANALYZING STRENGTHS, WEAKNESSES, AND PATHWAYS TO REFORM

Dr. Abdiweli M. Ali Gas
*Former Prime Minister of Somalia and
Former President of Puntland State of Somalia
Author: "A Challenging Transition in Somalia" Book*

How can a federal system be instituted in a fractured society reeling from a prolonged civil strife and a full-blown state collapse? Can this system help provide a constitutional relationship that is just and sustainable for the future generation of Somalia? How a decentralized federal system can address the pertinent issues of peace building and state building in Somalia? These questions and many more lie at the heart of Guled's manuscript **"Federalism Imperative in Post-Conflict Africa: The Case of Somalia."**

The study comprises of nine chapters and provides a holistic analysis of federalism in Somalia, its relevance for a conflict-prone country, its strength and weaknesses and proposed reforms. Drawing on the current literature in the field and on other federal arrangements in diverse countries, the author shows how an efficient system be instituted within the context of Somalia taking into account the quality of the country's institutions, the level of its political development, and the perceptions of its inhabitants of what federalism entails.

The author develops a cogent narrative that underlines the importance of federalism in Somalia, its devolution since its inception in early 2000, the main underlying weaknesses particularly recurrent conflicts arising between the central government and the federal members states. The study highlights the factors shaping federalism in Somalia. It draws special attention to seven factors which may negatively or positively affect discourse of federalism in Somalia. The book identifies how weak institutions and resource constraints hamper the implementation of federalism in Somalia. After all, good institutions beget good governance and much of political development in developing countries hinges on the strength of their institutional framework; hence as Dr. Guled's work suggests, federalism is not a panacea but a system predicated on the resources available and the quality of its basic institutions. It delivers only when the requisite conditions are met.

The author identifies seven tools and instruments that befits as guiding principles of federalism in Somalia. Among them are the provisional constitution, the laws and the regulations of the federal government, and the respective responsibilities of the center and the periphery. The author proffers and identifies steps needed to improve the federalization of the political system in Somalia such as the formation of the constitutional court and the delineation of the roles and responsibilities between the federal government and the federal member states. The importance of harmonized monetary and fiscal policies are also highlighted in the study.

One of the most important outcomes of Dr. Guled's study is the high level of awareness of federalism among the Somali people and as their preferred and suitable governance system for Somalia compared to decentralized or a unitary system on the backdrop of the bitter taste of Siyad Barre's dictatorial rule of 21 years where the power of the state was concentrated in the hands of one person, one entity, and one city.

The manuscript addressed the weaknesses in the current federal arrangement in Somalia including the lack of effective mechanism to resolve disputes between the federal government and the federal member states and the limited capacity and resources at the federal level among others. Finally the study presents reforms required to address and mitigate these weaknesses to make the federal system amiable to the current conditions in Somalia, including the completion of the constitutional review process and defined clear roles and responsibilities between the federal government and the federal member states, among others.

The conclusion of the study is, despite all its weaknesses and enduring challenges, federalism is the preferred governance system and has the potential for state-building and peace-building in Somalia. It is the most comprehensive scholarly work on federalism in Somalia. It will be a great addition and a good reference for future studies of federalism within the context of conflict-prone developing countries like Somalia. It is also a tool of analysis and a guide for the current political discourse in Somalia.

A BRIEF WORD ABOUT DR. GULED SALAH BARRE:

Dr. Barre was my colleague at Puntland State of Somalia. He served as a cabinet member and was the Minister of Environment during my tenure as the President of Puntland State of Somalia. Glued is a rising star in Somali politics and is one of the finest in the current crop of leaders in Somalia. As the Minister of Environment in the Puntland State of Somalia, he provided leadership and support for a struggling institution in a very difficult circumstance. He is also a first-rate academic with great versatility and a catching intellectual acumen. I saw first-hand his leadership skills. A charismatic leader, he was a great mentor to his subordinates and the ministerial staff. His passion for an effective public service was quite admirable. He was an exceptional member of my cabinet and I was fortunate to have him as my advisor and a close associate.

During his tenure as the Minister of Environment, he played a critical role in promoting environmental education in Puntland. He drafted and passed significant environmental bills including environment rehabilitation and drought mitigation bills which are instrumental on a socio-economic development based on livestock and agriculture. He was also a member of a legislative and executive team assembled to deal with the federal government on issues pertaining to federalism and the constitutional process taking place at the time. He was instrumental in these negotiations and in drafting a federal institutional framework that was critical in promoting reconciliation, stability, and good governance in Somalia.

FOREWORD

FROM IDEALISM TO POLITICAL REALISM: FEDERALISM AS A PATHWAY FOR SOMALI STATE-BUILDING

Prof. Abdurahman A. Baadiyow
Author: "Making Sense of Somali History" Book

I had the privilege of reviewing Dr. Guled Salah's manuscript, which was both an enjoyable and enlightening experience. Through this process, I gained valuable insights into federalism in general and the specific challenges associated with its implementation in Somalia. As a historian, I am well-versed in the history of Somali state failure, characterized by a centralized system with majoritarian democracy and authoritarian rule, culminating in its collapse in 1991. The Somali peace conferences held in Djibouti in 2000 and Kenya in 2004 laid the foundational paradigms for Somali state-building, marking a significant shift in governance. Subsequently, five federal member states and the Banadir region have been formalized, each with its regional administration. However, the issue of Somaliland persists, operating as a breakaway administration and maintaining its claim to independence, thereby functioning separately from the federal system.

The transition from centralized governance to federalism represents a significant paradigm shift in Somali state-building. Federalism emerged as a pivotal component of the constitutional-making process in 2004, complementing the clan power-sharing dynamics of the 4.5 formula and the incorporation of Islam as the ultimate legal reference, established during the Arta conference in 2000. These three elements signify a departure from the secularization, vilification of clan identity, and centralization adopted by the collapsed Somali state in 1991. Federalism allows for greater local autonomy, empowering regions to address their specific needs while fostering cooperation among various groups by distributing power more equitably. While federalism offers a viable pathway for Somali state-building, it has great challenges. Its successful implementation hinges on meeting several conditions and requires exceptional leadership with the right political culture. Such leadership must be committed to the equality of all citizens, the supremacy of the law, and national unity, recognizing federalism as a tool for fostering inclusivity and stability.

Somalia's state-building endeavors face significant internal challenges, notably establishing an appropriate governance system and developing a democratic process for nurturing qualified leadership. Federalism has been embraced to address these governance hurdles, facilitating regional participation in decision-making. Nonetheless, a substantial deficit exists in understanding federalism's intricacies, including its requisites, procedures, benefits, and obstacles. Dr. Guled Salah's book emerges as a pivotal resource, presenting a comprehensive examination of African federalism, with Somalia as a case study. It furnishes historical and theoretical contexts crucial for grasping federalism and conducts a comparative analysis across diverse contexts, spanning developed states, multinational entities, emerging economies, and post-conflict societies. The study identifies and evaluates five pivotal weaknesses in Somalia's federal governance framework: the absence of a clear definition, inadequate dispute resolution mechanisms, limited capacity and resources, unresolved pre-adoption agreements, and coordination challenges. Furthermore, it presents a holistic framework to enhance the efficacy of Somali federalism. This framework advocates for a clarified definition of federalism, establishing robust dispute-resolution mechanisms, capacity-building initiatives, consensus-building on critical issues, and enhanced coordination between the federal government and federal member states.

Dr. Guled Salah's book is a culmination of his vast experience and expertise in Somali governance and federalism. With roles such as former Minister of Puntland state, director of the SIDRA Institute, and head of the Transitional Puntland Electoral Commission (TPEC), Dr. Salah brings invaluable practical knowledge to his work. His extensive field research in various member states offers valuable insights, empirical research, and practical solutions, making the book indispensable for policymakers, scholars, and anyone interested in Somali federalism. Policymakers can utilize Dr. Salah's insights to develop informed, context-specific strategies for governance improvement in Somalia. Moreover, the book can be integrated into the curriculum of university political science students, offering them a comprehensive understanding of federalism, particularly in post-conflict and emerging states. I strongly recommend that readers utilize this invaluable academic study, as it provides essential tools and knowledge for policymakers, scholars, students, and practitioners to contribute meaningfully to ongoing state-building efforts in Somalia.

PREFACE

Somalia's narrative, resonating with the experiences of many African nations, is steeped in the arduous quest for unity and stability following its emancipation from colonial rule. The year 1991 marked a pivotal turn in its history, witnessing the collapse of the central government, which plunged the nation into a tumultuous era of civil war and political upheaval. In this landscape of uncertainty and fragmented efforts at national reconciliation, the concept of federalism emerged as a beacon of hope. In 2004, Somali leaders, in a collective and historic move, embraced federalism, a decision that was legally solidified with the adoption of the provisional constitution in 2012. This bold step initiated the formation of federal member states and aimed to weave a tapestry of harmonious and efficient governance, fostering synergy between federal and state entities and championing inclusive representation across all societal spectrums.

My personal foray into the depths of Somalia's federalism commenced during my tenure from 2014 to 2015 as a cabinet minister in the government of Puntland, a key federal member state. This position offered me an unparalleled opportunity to engage with the intricate and often challenging realities of implementing federalism in a country as complex as Somalia. A notable aspect of my role was my involvement in a pivotal task force dedicated to navigating and ameliorating the strained relationship between Puntland and the Federal Government of Somalia. The depths of these negotiations and the intricate interplay of federal–state dynamics ignited a deep-seated interest in the broader framework and potential of federalism.

I consider myself to be one of the most ardent supporters of democratization in Somalia. From 2019 to 2022 I coordinated the first peaceful, free, and fair local elections in Somalia after more than fifty years. I learned the hard lesson that too much focus is placed on the mechanics of elections at the expense of more urgent issues: instilling the culture of democracy and the rule of law, developing progressive electoral laws and policies, promoting free speech and social reconciliation, and fighting corruption.

This nascent interest blossomed into a rigorous academic pursuit as I embarked on my PhD. Eager to dissect and understand the multifaceted nature of federalism in diverse geopolitical climates, I began a scholarly journey through the nuances of global federalism models. My aim was to extract and contextualize principles that would resonate most effectively with the unique political, social, and economic landscape of Somalia.

The Federalism Imperative in Post-Conflict Africa: The Case of Somalia represents a significant milestone in the ongoing discourse on governance in post-conflict settings, particularly on the African continent. This book is not merely a scholarly exploration of federalism; it is an extensive compilation of first-hand observations, rigorous research, and a dedicated commitment to understanding and explaining how federal structures can be implemented effectively in the challenging context of Somalia—a nation striving to reconstruct its social, political, and economic fabrics after decades of conflict.

This work delves deeply into the intricacies of adopting a federal system in environments marked by complex inter-tribal dynamics and historical grievances. It addresses the delicate balance required to administer governance that is both inclusive and effective, promoting unity without suppressing the rich cultural diversity that defines the Somali identity. This book methodically unpacks the layers of federal governance, analyzing their potential as catalysts for political stability and economic revival.

Each chapter of the book draws from a diverse range of successful federations around the world and is crafted with the intent to provide not only theoretical insights but also practical recommendations. This study highlights the unique challenges faced by Somalia, from the reconciliation of divided communities to the establishment of cooperative political structures that empower local leadership while ensuring a cohesive national strategy.

With immense pride and a profound sense of accomplishment, I am delighted to present *The Federalism Imperative in Post-Conflict Africa: The Case of Somalia.* This book offers a deep dive into the pivotal role of federalism in nation-building, drawing extensively from my personal experiences and research. It serves as a comprehensive guide for policymakers, scholars, and stakeholders involved in post-conflict recovery and outlines how federalism can enhance democratic governance, stimulate economic growth, and foster social cohesion. Specifically focusing on Somalia, it explores how federal structures can be adapted to meet the unique challenges faced by post-conflict African states, not just ensuring their survival but also promoting their prosperity. This book aims to spark a broader conversation on federal governance and stands as an essential resource for anyone committed to complex governance reform.

INTRODUCTION

The *Federalism Imperative in Post-Conflict Africa: The Case of Somalia* begins with a comprehensive overview of federalism, a governance system and power-sharing mechanism supporting 40% of the world's population living in federal states. This figure rises above 70% when broader decentralized governance structures are considered. Beyond being a governance model, federalism encompasses various sociopolitical benefits such as fostering national identity, promoting self-preservation, encouraging inter-state collaboration, and ensuring equitable resource distribution.

This book delves into the African context, where six nations, including Somalia, are recognized for their federal systems. However, research on African federal systems remains limited. Drawing from global experiences, we understand that successful federalism hinges on robust democratic institutions rooted in the rule of law. Yet understanding its effectiveness—which is deeply influenced by local political, social, and economic conditions—necessitates country-specific studies.

By exploring federalism within post-conflict settings and the African landscape, this study illuminates the intricacies of Somali federalism. It aims to guide effective implementation in Somalia and contributes to the broader discourse on federalism in similar contexts. Building on existing research since Somalia's adoption of federalism in 2004, this book navigates the challenges and potentials, extracting lessons and best practices from culturally and socioeconomically akin countries.

Somalia's journey toward federalism commenced in 2004 when, after various unsuccessful attempts to form a stable national government, the country's leaders recognized it as the optimal system. This initiative led to the creation of the Transitional Federal Government and, later, to the embedding of federalism in Somalia's Provisional Federal Constitution in 2012. Despite state-building challenges, significant strides have been made in the implementation of federalism, signaling a move toward reestablishing a fledgling governance system.

Primarily derived from my extensive PhD research, this book addresses gaps in the existing literature on Somalia's federalism. It aims to analyze the federal governance system in Somalia by drawing lessons and best practices from other post-conflict contexts to enhance peace-building and governance processes. It is based on a study spanning the period from the establishment of the Transitional Federal Government in 2004, a pivotal moment indicating Somalia's commitment to federal governance, to 2022. This period was characterized by significant efforts to implement federal governance structures.

Located in the Horn of Africa, Somalia covers an area of 637,657 square kilometers and is bordered by Djibouti, Ethiopia, and Kenya. Its coastline of 3,333 kilometers is the second longest in Africa. The study encompassed six of Somalia's regions: all five existing federal member states—Jubaland, Galmudug, Hirshabelle, Southwest, and Puntland—as well as the Banadir region, which hosts the federal government. Not included in this study is Somaliland, a region that operates autonomously from the federal structure but engages in collaborative activities with the rest of Somalia.

Methodologically, the study adopted a mixed-methods approach that relied primarily on a review of secondary data through a comprehensive desk review of relevant research, studies, and reports. This preliminary review informed the research design and helped shape the primary data collection strategy, which included key informant interviews (KIIs), focus group discussions (FGDs), and a survey of the public.

Data collection occurred from May 2021 to April 2022 to obtain a comprehensive view of the current state of federal governance in

Somalia. Field data collection tools were meticulously developed, tested, and validated. The KIIs and FGDs were initiated first and their findings were used to refine the focus of the subsequent public survey. Two FGDs were conducted, with participants selected to represent a diverse cross-section of society, including women, youth, business leaders, and community members. Fifteen key informants were selected across four clusters—government staff and politicians (five), traditional elders and clan leaders (three), judiciary staff and constitutional lawyers (four), and international community and development partners (three)—to provide in-depth insights into the federalism process in Somalia.

The public survey utilized a two-stage stratified cluster design, targeting the capitals of the five federal member states and the Banadir Regional Administration, which is the Mogadishu metropolitan area, the capital of the Republic of Somalia. A total of 384 respondents were randomly selected for the public survey; they were drawn from the six regions and represented various societal segments, including government, civil society, academia, and the private sector. This approach ensured a balanced and representative sample across the surveyed regions.

This methodology not only captured the complexities inherent in Somalia's federal system but also positioned the study to offer actionable insights for improving governance and peace-building efforts in similar post-conflict settings. By scrutinizing the strengths and weaknesses of the federalist governance system at federal and state levels, this study identified necessary reforms for efficient governance. Additionally, it assessed the impact of federalism on Somalia's political, social, and economic development across four domains. These domains—the contextual factors influencing federalism—comprise the guiding tools, public awareness about federalism, and the challenges and opportunities within the current federal governance structure. This study proposes effective frameworks for federalism and state building.

The findings of this study highlight the intricate interplay between federal frameworks and local conditions in Somalia, detailing both significant achievements and ongoing challenges within the federal system. This analysis emphasizes the crucial role of effective intergovernmental coordination in navigating complex political and socioeconomic landscapes, shaped by diverse regional demands and national goals. The research underscores the necessity for adaptable legal frameworks that ensure transparency and uphold accountability throughout the levels of government. Furthermore, the study stresses the importance of extensive public engagement and advocates for comprehensive programs of civic education. These initiatives are essential for fostering an informed citizenry ready to participate actively in the federal governance process, thereby boosting democratic participation and effective governance.

By concentrating on these critical areas, the study offers a comprehensive framework that serves as both a blueprint for assessing and enhancing the key elements of federalism in Somalia and a catalyst for vital discussions on customizing the federal system to Somalia's unique historical, social, and political landscape. This strategic approach is designed to deepen the institutionalization and effectiveness of federalism, ensuring it aligns with the nation's specific needs and contributes positively to its developmental objectives. The framework encourages ongoing refinement and adaptation while emphasizing the importance of local context in the successful implementation of federal structures. It aims to foster a more cohesive and responsive governance system that effectively addresses both current challenges and future opportunities.

By providing new insights into federalism, particularly in contexts akin to Somalia, this study contributes substantially to the theory and practice of federalism as a state-building tool and governance system. The findings, conclusions, and recommendations of this study are expected to stimulate novel thinking and to guide strategies to effectively implement federalism, thereby transforming Somalia's political, social, and economic fabric.

Introduction

This book, comprising nine chapters, is neatly organized into two main parts:

Part 1 encompasses Chapters 1 through 3, setting the stage with a global perspective on federalism. Chapter 1 delves into the historical roots and evolution of federalism to provide a comprehensive background. Chapter 2 offers a comparative analysis, exploring how federalism operates across twelve countries that range from established democracies to nations rebuilding after conflict. The focus then shifts to Africa in Chapter 3, where the unique dynamics and applications of federalism on the continent are examined in depth.

Part 2, which encompasses Chapters 4 through 9, narrows the focus to Somalia and offers a detailed exploration of federalism in this specific context. Chapter 4 lays the groundwork by discussing the conceptual, historical, and constitutional foundations of Somali federalism. Chapter 5 examines the factors influencing the shape and practice of federalism in Somalia, while Chapter 6 scrutinizes the tools and policies that have directed its course. Chapter 7 evaluates the Somali people's understanding of federalism and its impact on various societal aspects. Chapter 8 identifies the challenges within the current federal structure, suggesting necessary reforms. The book concludes with Chapter 9, which synthesizes the research findings and presents key recommendations. This final chapter offers strategic insights, drawn from the extensive analysis conducted in the preceding chapters, to propose forward-looking solutions for the advancement and effective implementation of federalism in Somalia. This structure ensures a comprehensive understanding of federalism from a broad perspective before focusing on its specific application in Somalia.

PART 1

THE EVOLUTION *of* FEDERALISM: HISTORICAL & CONTEMPORARY PERSPECTIVES

This part delves into the evolution and contemporary impact of federalism, examining its core principles, and its role in democracy, politics, and conflict resolution. It assesses both the strengths and challenges of federal systems and uses comparative analysis to show how federalism operates across different global contexts, including established democracies, multinational states, emerging economies, and post-conflict societies. Special emphasis is placed on post-conflict African nations, evaluating how federalism supports peace, stability, and development through its institutional frameworks and its effects on political, social, and economic progress.

CHAPTER 1

HISTORY & CONCEPT *of* FEDERALISM: A COMPREHENSIVE OVERVIEW

1.1. INTRODUCTION

Federalism boasts a diverse and intricate history, having evolved over centuries to align with the changing political, social, and economic landscapes of various societies around the world. This system of governance is fundamentally based on a balance of power, delicately distributed between a central authority and its constituent units. This balance is essential, as it marries the principles of unity and diversity, allowing for a harmonious coexistence of varied regional identities within a singular national framework. This chapter examines the historical progression of federalism, exploring its conceptual roots and how these foundational ideas have shaped its adoption and adaptation in differing global settings.

Throughout its evolution, federalism has demonstrated remarkable versatility, adapting to the unique requirements of diverse societies. From the federations of ancient times to the complex federal structures we see today, its evolution reflects an ongoing adaptation to societal needs, regional peculiarities, and historical contexts. This exploration examines the nuances and transformations of federalism to understand how it has been employed as a governance model across various cultures and epochs. By tracing its development and observing its global manifestations, this chapter provides a comprehensive overview of federalism's role in shaping governance structures, highlighting its capacity to effectively blend regional autonomy with national unity.

1.2. DEFINING EDERALISM

The word "federal" emanates from the Latin word *foedus*, which means covenant, treaty, agreement, or league[1]. It typifies the ideas of promise, commitment, and undertaking, which consequently include the ideas of cooperation, reciprocity, and mutuality[2]. An early scholar of federalism, Professor Kenneth C. Wheare, in his seminal book *Federal Government*, defined federalism—or what he called at the time the "federal principle"—as "the method of dividing powers so that the general and regional governments are each, within a sphere, coordinate and independent"[3]. Since then, some scholars have attempted to broaden the theoretical explanation of federalism to encompass the historical, political, structural, and institutional context of the different types of federalism. Others have tried to construct a narrower definition that returns to the basic principle of federalism—that of power separation, coordination, and the sharing of sovereignty rights[4].

Elazar promoted a broader perspective on federalism, one beyond the definition of the structural arrangement of the political system. He wrote that "federalism is more than an arrangement of government structures; it is a mode of political activity that requires certain kinds of cooperative relationships through the political system it animates"[5]. He argued that the debate between centralized and federated systems of government highlights a fundamental divide in the perception of civil society, distinguishing between what he terms the "systematic" and "prismatic" approaches. Elazar noted that advocates of centralism focus on sovereignty as a critical means of establishing definitive boundaries. In contrast, supporters of federalism emphasize the need to recognize multiple distinct cores within a society, advocating for a nuanced approach that tailors responses to the unique needs and perspectives of each segment. In short, Elazar supported the understand-

---

1 Wheare, 1946
2 Elazar, 1987
3 Wheare, 1946:11
4 Elazar, 1987
5 Elazar, 1987:2

ing of federalism as multiple polities related to one another, united and yet separate.

Perspectives that frame federalism in legal and constitutional frameworks as the mere separation of powers between two levels of government would be too simplistic. They fail to consider important components of federalism—such as social issues, ethnic and national identity, loyalty, self-preservation and localism—as well as such governance issues as intergovernmental collaboration, power and resource sharing, decision-making, legitimacy and democracy.

Federalism is the constitutional division of sovereign governmental power between multiple levels of government. It is one of the mechanisms of power sharing aimed at having states or provinces that are able to address their own challenges to use their available resources as defined by their specificity. Federal states are usually made up of non-overlapping and partially independent subnational jurisdictions defined on the basis of geographical location rather than on function[6]. Therefore, in a real sense, federalism (culture, demography, migrations, and history) is widely accepted as a tool for promoting a variety of normative goods. These goods include, for example, democratic politics, efficient and shared governance, and liberty and union among state and national players as well as cooperation and competition for sustainable development.

At its core, federalism is anchored in three fundamental principles: shared sovereignty, the division of powers, and robust intergovernmental relations.

Sovereignty: The essence of federalism lies in its foundation of shared sovereignty. Unlike other forms of governance where sovereignty is held exclusively at the center, federalism embraces a constitutional division of sovereignty between different levels of government. Both the central and regional governments maintain authority over their distinct domains, which fosters a dual-sovereignty structure. This unique characteristic of federalism allows for a

---

6 Feeley and Rubin, 2011

balance of power, ensuring that both national and regional interests are represented and safeguarded.

Division of Powers: Central to the concept of federalism is a clearly delineated division of powers between the central and regional governments, a division typically enshrined in a country's constitution. This separation of powers allocates certain responsibilities and authorities—such as defense, foreign affairs, and currency management—to the federal government while reserving other responsibilities— including education, healthcare, and local development initiatives—for regional governments,. Moreover, certain powers are concurrent, shared between the two levels. This structured division not only promotes efficiency and unity at the national level but also encourages diversity and self-governance at the regional level. It serves as a system of checks and balances, preventing the concentration of power and thereby protecting the rights of individuals and regions.

Intergovernmental Relations: A pivotal element of federalism is the dynamic of intergovernmental relations, which dictates the interactions between different levels of government. To function effectively, a federal system requires established mechanisms for coordination and cooperation between the central and regional governments. These mechanisms can take various forms, from formal institutions like intergovernmental councils to more informal practices characterized by collaborative federalism. The quality of these intergovernmental relations is crucial in managing areas of overlapping responsibility, addressing issues that span different levels of governance, and facilitating effective dispute resolution. They are integral to ensuring that policy-making within a federal framework is cohesive and takes into account the diverse needs and perspectives of the various constituencies.

Federalism often contrasts with unitary and confederal governance forms. In unitary systems, the central government holds supreme authority, with regional or local governments operating under its control. Such systems, common in countries with smaller territories or less regional diversity, feature a centralized decision-making process with limited regional autonomy[7]. Conversely, a confederal system represents a loose alliance of independent states, where the central authority is weak, and constituent units maintain significant sovereignty. The European Union partially exemplifies a confederation, with member states retaining substantial sovereignty while delegating certain powers to EU institutions[8].

Thus, federal systems find a balance between the highly centralized unitary system and the loosely connected confederal system. In federalism, central and regional governments independently exercise their authority within their respective realms, united under a constitution that defines their powers and duties. This arrangement fosters regional diversity and local decision-making within a cohesive national framework[9].

However, a number of contentious questions have arisen in the quest for federalism and are of particular importance to political theorists and analysts. First, there have been many criticisms of the portrayal of federalism as an advantageous system of government and its purported values as being the best political arrangement for accommodating ethnic, cultural, and religious diversity, for promoting social cohesion, democratization and decentralization, and as a way of bringing governance closer to local people. Second, the manner in which power is shared in a federal system of governance creates complex and multi-layered levels as well as legal and institutional intricacies, especially considering the divisions and devolutions of power between states and national governments. Third, the sustainability of federalism system in resource-limited contexts and in countries with weak institutions is frequently questioned[10].

---

7 Elazar, 1987
8 MacCormick, 1995
9 Stepan, 1999
10 Anderson, 2008

1.3. HISTORICAL ORIGINS AND EVOLUTION OF FEDERALISM

Federalism is not a recent phenomenon, but can be traced back to ancient civilizations, when cities and states joined to form alliances for mutual defense against the conquest ambitions of strong empires such as Macedonia, Rome, and Sparta[11]. But contemporary federalism dates back to the formation of the United States of America in 1787; this is considered to be the oldest and most successful modern constitutional federal polity. In contrast to the tactics used in forming ancient alliances and unification approaches, today's federalism is considered in the context of decentralization, devolution of power and resources to the local level, and democratization.

The nature and functioning of federal systems of government have evolved over the centuries from the pioneering experiment of the United States to today's diverse federal structures that are characterized not only as political concepts but also in terms of their structural, legal, social, and institutional attributes as well as their processes and practices.

The United States' establishment of a federal system upon the ratification of its constitution in 1788 marked a critical turning point in the history of federalism. The US model, influenced by the inadequacies of the Articles of Confederation, introduced a dual system of government where sovereignty was divided between the national and state governments. This system, detailed in *The Federalist Papers* by Hamilton, Jay and Madison, sought to balance the need for a robust central authority with the preservation of state autonomy, setting a precedent for other nations.

In Europe, federalism developed differently, often emerging as a response to the need to unify diverse cultural, linguistic, and regional entities under a single national framework. Switzerland's adoption of federalism in 1848, a response to deep linguistic and cultural divides, creatied a confederation where cantons retained significant

---

[11] Bataveljić, 2012

autonomy. Similarly, Germany's federal structure, forged in the aftermath of World War II, represented a commitment to unifying various states while ensuring representation and autonomy for each.

In the twentieth century, federalism became the preferred model for many newly independent nations seeking to accommodate diverse ethnic, linguistic, and regional groups within a single national framework. Countries like India, Nigeria, and Brazil adopted federal structures to manage their complex internal diversities and foster unity. Each of these countries tailored the federal model to suit their unique historical and social contexts.

Table 1 lists of countries with federal systems of government
(Griffith, Chattopadhyay, Light and Stieren, 2020)
the six federal countries in Africa are highlighted light grey.

Country	Population	Government Structure
Argentina	45,212,784	The executive, a bicameral legislative branch, 23 provinces, and the autonomous City of Buenos Aires
Australia	25,512,139	The central government (called the Commonwealth), federal parliament, six states, and two self-governing mainland territories: the Northern Territory and the Australian Capital Territory
Austria	9,008,348	The executive, a bicameral legislative branch, and nine states (known as Länder)
Belgium	11,591,663	The executive, a bicameral legislative branch, three communities (the two regions of Flemish and Wallonia), and the capital city, Brussels
Bosnia and Herzegovina	3,279,859	The executive, a bicameral legislative branch, and three constituent entities: Bosnia, Herzegovina and Republika Srpska
Brazil	212,620,512	Three levels of government: the central government (the executive and a two-chamber legislative branch), 26 states and federal district government, and 5,500 municipal governments

Country	Population	Government Structure
Canada	37,755,834	The executive, a bicameral legislative branch, ten provinces, and three territories
Comoros	870,366	The executive, a unicameral legislative branch, and three autonomous islands
Ethiopia	115,081,818	The executive, a bicameral legislative branch, nine autonomous regions, and two chartered cities
Germany	83,792,897	The executive, a bicameral legislative branch, 15 regions (Länder), and Berlin
India	1,380,562,295	The executive, a bicameral legislative branch, 28 states, and 7 union territories
Iraq	40,261,733	The executive, a unicameral legislative branch, and 19 provinces
Malaysia	32,382,844	The executive, a bicameral legislative branch, 13 states, and 3 federal territories
Mexico	128,988,493	The executive, a bicameral legislative branch, and 31 states
Federated States of Micronesia	115,068	The executive, a unicameral legislative branch, and four states
Nepal	29,155,873	The executive, a bicameral legislative branch, and 7 provinces
Nigeria	206,352,214	The executive, a bicameral legislative branch, 36 states, and the federal capital territory, Abuja
Pakistan	221,068,260	The executive, federal parliament, four provinces, one federal capital territory, two self-governing administrative territories and a unit of semi-autonomous federally administered tribal areas
Papua New Guinea	8,954,480	Federal constitutional monarchy: the executive, a unicameral legislative branch, 18 provinces, the autonomous Region of Bougainville, and the National Capital District

Country	Population	Government Structure
Russia	145,936,517	The executive, a bicameral legislative branch, and eighty-five federal subjects of six different types
St. Kitts and Nevis	53,199	The executive, a unicameral national assembly, and a separate national assembly for Nevis Island
South Africa	59,339,500	The executive, a bicameral legislative branch and nine provinces
Somalia	15,911,717	The executive, a bicameral legislative branch, five federal member states, the capital, and Somaliland
Spain	46,754,613	The executive, a bicameral legislative branch, 17 autonomous communities, and two autonomous cities
Sudan	43,894,567	The executive, a bicameral legislative branch, and 18 states
Switzerland	8,657,307	Three levels of governance with each executive and legislative powers: Confederation (central state), the 26 cantons (the federal states), and the 2,352 communes
United Arab Emirates	9,894,917	Federal monarchy: the executive (Federal Supreme Council, President and Vice President, and the Cabinet), the unicameral legislative branch (Federal National Council) and 7 constituent monarchies (self-administering emirates)
United States of America	331,083,426	The executive, a bicameral legislative branch, and 50 states, one federal district (Washington, DC), one incorporated territory (Palmyra Atoll), and the unincorporated territory (Puerto Rico)
Venezuela	28,437,830	The executive, a unicameral legislative branch, 23 states, one Capital District, and the Federal Dependencies

The history of federalism unfolds as a narrative marked by constant evolution and adaptation. It traces a path from deep philosophical roots to practical implementation in various nations, each shaping the concept to suit its unique cultural, political, and social fabric. As a governance model, federalism has demonstrated remarkable versatility, providing solutions to the challenges of managing diverse, pluralistic societies. It has evolved from a theoretical concept discussed by political philosophers to a tangible system adopted by nations seeking to balance the delicate interplay between national unity and regional diversity[12].

In its early manifestations, federalism sought to address the needs of disparate communities and regions, fostering cooperation while maintaining distinct identities. Over centuries, this system has been refined and redefined, adapting to the nuances of different historical eras and geopolitical contexts. Modern federalism, as seen in countries like the United States, Germany, and Australia, reflects a sophisticated understanding of governance, where power is strategically shared and distributed to ensure efficiency, representation, and stability[13].

As the global landscape continues to grow in complexity, with heightened interdependence among nations and increasing internal diversity, the principles of federalism are likely to undergo further evolution. This evolution will be driven by the need to strike an optimal balance between central authority and regional autonomy, catering to both national priorities and regional preferences. The future of federalism hinges on its ability to remain flexible and responsive to emerging challenges, such as globalization, technological advancements, and shifting demographic patterns[14].

In this context, federalism will not only have to accommodate traditional concepts of territorial governance but also adapt to new forms of cultural and economic diversification. As societies continue to change, federal structures may need to become more fluid and innovative, potentially incorporating digital governance mechanisms

---

12 Elazar, 1987
13 Watts, 2007
14 Fenna and Thomas, 2015

and addressing transnational issues. This ongoing evolution of federalism stands as a testament to its enduring relevance, highlighting its role as a dynamic, adaptable governance model well-suited to navigate the complexities of the modern world.

1.4. PHILOSOPHICAL BASIS: UNITY AND DIVERSITY

The philosophical underpinnings of federalism lie in its ability to harmonize the dual concepts of unity and diversity within a political system. This framework is designed to acknowledge and preserve the social, political, cultural, and religious differences of distinct constituent units (diversity), while concurrently weaving these disparate entities into a cohesive and representative political entity (unity). Federalism is not ideologically rigid in favoring either states or the federal government. Instead, it aims to moderate the influence of the federal government in state affairs, thereby safeguarding the autonomy of the constituent units.

Conversely, the rights of states to maintain autonomy in various domains are counterpoised with the necessity to cede certain powers to the national government and to adhere to federal laws. The theoretical foundation of federalism seeks to mediate conflicts among constituent units, preventing stalemate, disengagement, and further conflict. In this sense, federalism can be viewed through the lens of the Westphalian principle of sovereignty and authority, emphasizing the need to avert rivalry and conflict through pragmatic reasoning and recognizing the equality of different government levels within the federal structure. This theory of federalism posits that while ultimate sovereignty resides with the federal government, states or regional entities also exercise sovereignty rights, particularly in cooperative federal systems. This notion aligns federalism with the Westphalian concept in practical modeling and institutional design, countering central government hegemony and promoting coexistence. Federal structures establish coordinate levels of government, each respecting the other's legitimate governance rights and encouraging intergovernmental cooperation.

Some scholars have interpreted federalism as a form of Westphalian liberalism, wherein it safeguards the liberties of individuals, subnational governments, and the national government. Hills (2006) articulates the idea that commitment to federalism entails a commitment to protecting private liberty. This approach to federalism is aimed at diverting attention from divisive disagreements toward decision-making processes that enjoy a broader societal consensus, thereby fostering a more harmonious and unified governance structure.

1.5. FEDERALISM, DEMOCRACY AND POLITICS

Chevreau (2019) demonstrates that federalism studies have evolved from focusing on its institutional and legal aims to looking at its broad aims and associated complex social and political relationships and interactions. Geographical, historical, economic, ideological, security, intellectual, cultural, demographic, and international factors all contribute to unity or regional diversity. These factors influence the consideration of different military, federal, or non-federal governance alternatives and influence their operation.

Chevreau (2019) has observed that different federal systems have witnessed a degree of elite accommodation in negotiation among political parties and in public involvement. Federalism studies have noted that established federal systems are dynamic and continue to evolve—some move toward centralization while others move toward decentralization, depending on the interaction of social, political, and ethnic factors.

As federal systems have evolved from a legal and institutional focus, constitutions have played a vital role in the establishment of federal systems. There is enormous variation in the form and scope through which constitutional power is distributed in federations, and there is no single index that can be used to measure the extent of autonomous decisions of federal states or of co-decisions at the federal government level.

Notwithstanding, federations are characterized as decentralized political systems. The distinction between "decentralization" and "non-decentralization" is important. While decentralization implies hierarchy of power from the center to the peripheral, "non-centralization" implies the constitutionally structured disposition of powers. Non-centralization therefore better represents the essential power of federalism.

According to Chevreau, another important concept is that of intergovernmental relations. These relations are due to the nature of overlap and interdependence as different levels of government exercise their responsibilities; success in a federal system depends a great deal on intergovernmental consultation, cooperation, and coordination. Intergovernmental relations present other challenges that include reduction in flexibility due to joint decisions and loss of democratic accountability that could result from intergovernmental collusion.

Regarding revenue, in practice it is impossible to assign autonomous revenue sources to each government that will match its expenditure responsibilities. Even if such matching were attained, it would shift over time due to differences in tax value and expenditure costs. Therefore, federal systems must resort to a variety of financial transfers to correct ongoing imbalances vertically between different orders of government and horizontally between different contingents because of their differences in capacities and expenditures.

The relation between federalism and democracy is complex, but by its nature federalism promotes democracy. In particular, federal systems advocate for democracy by promoting self-rule and enhancing self-rule through several levels of government. Also, shared rule brings together disparate social, economic, ethnic, and religious interests.

Chevreau notes that federal systems facilitate political integration, democratic development, and economic effectiveness better than do non-federal systems. Although total equality among the constituent units in a federal system introduces complexity and problems that may be severe, in some cases a federal system has proved necessary to accommodate and address varied regional differences.

The cumulative reinforcement of political division results in development of increasingly polarizing processes that undermine tolerance and compromise. Chevreau's study draws the following key conclusions: (i) federal political systems provide practical ways to combine the benefits of unity and diversity but are not a solution to all political problems; and (ii) success of federal systems depends to a large degree on public acceptance of the need to respect constitutional norms and structures and on a prevailing spirit of tolerance and compromise.

In the case of Rwanda, state building and conflict resolution have been managed by use of decentralization systems with consideration for the demands of different regions of the country and for the norms and customs with which the communities identify[15]. Therefore, the acceptance of the devolution of power and authority has helped the government to push its national development initiatives with ease. Subnational governments also have control over some resources, although in Rwanda some devolutionary activities have been successful even without citizens' acceptance[16].

Chevreau points out that there are enormous varieties in the application of the federal idea. He notes that the success of federal systems seems to depend on how well they can accommodate evolving political realities by championing a federal variant that adequately expresses the circumstances and needs of a particular society at a given time in history. Most federations have included in their constitution a set of fundamental rights. Others have additional provisions to protect minorities and the most marginalized.

---

15 Paine, 2019
16 Martinez-Vazquez, 2003

1.6. FEDERALISM, CONFLICT AND PEACE SETTINGS

States use federalism to manage preexisting diversity. Since most violent conflicts occur between groups within a country, federalism provides an effective means to accommodate different groups, protect minorities, maintain political stability, and prevent disintegration. Therefore, federalism gives regions the autonomy of "self-rule" while they participate, influence, and make decisions within the center's "shared rule"; this avoids fragmentation or the break-up of the state.

Chevreau (2019) examines the strength and reality of federalism as an appropriate and effective approach to peace building and state building in fragile and conflict-affected states. He compares federalism to the alternatives of consociation and a decentralized unitary state. The key features of federalism include: (i) at least two tiers of government endowed with sovereign power on some matter; (ii) an amendable, supreme, written constitution with vertical and horizontal division of power; (iii) representation mechanisms for self-rule and shared rule; and (iv) an umpire. Federal systems vary widely in their objectives, in the way they are formed, and in their successes and failures.

One school of thought[17] argues that federalism is the best instrument to promote cooperation between opposing groups, empower local groups, and set up effective institutions. Another group, for example Hueglin (2003), argues that federalism has shortfalls, creates social divisions, and is difficult to implement in post-conflict situations where local and national institutions are weak.

Chevreau (2019) observes that classical federalism has been implemented in developed countries like Canada where federal and provincial governments operate independently of each other in their own respective areas of jurisdiction. To succeed, a federal system should meet the economic and political goals of all stakeholders but many scholars, such as Elazar (1987) agree that the structure of the

---

17 Elazar, 1987

adopted federal system plays an important role in determining its success.

Watts (2007) observes that federal systems may be established at once or in stages and may involve aggregation, devolution, or a mix of both. Watts identifies cooperative and competitive federalism as additional concepts that have been revealed in federalism. Political parties, which play an important role in the political dynamics of a federation, reinforce intergovernmental cooperation and competition. For example, in their study of the role of political parties in conflict resolution in Nepal, Dahal and Bhatta (2008) conclude that a political system without political parties is like playing football with no teams to compete. Political parties act as tools used by different political opponents to portray new programs and reforms for the benefit of their states. Hence they promote service delivery, one of the aims of devolving functions, by running a federation. Political parties also act as organized vehicles through which people can collectively voice their demands to be addressed by the government.

Anderson and Keil (2018) note that federalism has been one of the international community's preferred tools for conflict resolution and peace building. This is due to its ability to satisfy the aspirations and needs of both majority and minority groups. Anderson and Keil suggest that federalism is an attractive tool in post-conflict settings because it allows division of power and resources among different groups while maintaining overall national integrity. It allows different groups to have control over specific interests' such as social and cultural issues while they participate and influence national decisions and policies.

Chevreau (2019) claims that federalism has been promoted as an effective governance system in ethnically divided post-conflict states because it: (i) enables sustainable power sharing between communities with ethnic and cultural differences; (ii) allows individual communities to determine how they want to be governed within their region; and (iii) limits the ability of the central government to repress and control the development of particular groups or communities.

1.7. FEDERALISM AS INTERSYSTEM GOVERNANCE

Schapiro posits federalism as "inter-systemic governance" (2007:115). He describes the reality in federalism that the laws promulgated in one level of government effect the other level. Similarly, "a regulated entity, be it a person, a corporation, or a political subdivision, finds its conduct controlled by the laws of more than one political authority"[18]. Schapiro plays down the argument around establishing political, legal, and administrative boundaries between the state and federal governments, saying that "an account of the appropriate roles of the states and the federal government cannot turn on an analysis of whether a subject is 'truly local' or 'truly national'" 2007:124). In contemporary societies, the dichotomy of "truly local" and "truly national" has no substance. Schapiro says "the existence of multiple, overlapping legal regimes is a pervasive feature of contemporary society" (2007:121). He explains federalism from a different perspective that he calls a "polyphonic approach." This approach "emphasizes that, as a descriptive matter, states and the federal government in fact exercise extensive concurrent authority" and emphasizes the importance of managing effectively "the overlap and interaction of state and federal power"[19].

Schapiro's inter-systemic governance federalism may appear to diverge from the traditional Westphalian model, wherein a nation-state possesses exclusive sovereign authority and complete control. He observes that democratic federalism shares the principles of Westphalian democracy in which citizens have control over their laws and leaders through democratic pressure and mechanisms that allow them, if dissatisfied, to change the laws or the leaders. However, he argues that "in a contemporary setting of inter-systemic governance, this story of Westphalian democratic legitimacy no longer applies with full force. Laws promulgated by one polity have effect

---

18 Schapiro, 2007:122
19 Schapiro, 2007:118

in other polities. Many factors account for the increasingly porous nature of legal boundaries"[20].

Another interesting aspect of Schapiro's polyphonic approach is its rejection of attempts to separate state and federal involvements as two inherently distinctive polities. If the levels of governments are considered as one and the sovereignty is treated as a shared responsibility, federalism could accommodate the Westphalian principle. It is worth mentioning that the dual-federalism approach took a different perspective to align with the Westphalian theory of government in that it attempted "to preserve a Westphalian conception of sovereignty by making states sovereign in their own spheres, while the federal government enjoyed exclusive authority in others"[21].

Anderson and Keil (2018) observe two dimensions of federalism—that it is a governance principle on one hand, and an institutional reality of a federal state on the other. Federalism gives both majority and minority groups control over their own economic, political, and social affairs while ensuring the territorial integrity of the larger state. According to Anderson and Keil, the states rescind some of their sovereignty to pull resources together to form a larger network.

1.8. CRITICISMS AND LIMITATIONS OF FEDERALISM

Federalism, although providing a structure for balancing power and accommodating diversity, faces a range of criticisms and limitations that often stem from its inherent complexity. This complexity can lead to bureaucratic complications and inefficiencies, particularly in modern political and social contexts.

A significant criticism of federalism lies in its intrinsic complexity, with power divided among various levels of government, resulting in bureaucratic complexities and overlapping responsibilities. This can lead to confusion, duplicated efforts, and inefficiencies in policy

---

20 Schapiro, 2007:123
21 Schapiro, 2007:127

execution. The United States exemplifies this challenge, where the interplay of federal, state, and local governments creates a labyrinthine regulatory environment, often resulting in inconsistent law enforcement and policy implementation. Furthermore, federalism can struggle with agile governance during crises, as seen in the US response to Hurricane Katrina, where the multi-tiered government structure impeded effective disaster relief[22].

Achieving a suitable balance between national unity and regional autonomy presents another challenge in federal systems. Overcentralization can neglect unique cultural or political regions, while excessive decentralization may weaken the central government's ability to enforce uniform national policies. This dynamic equilibrium requires ongoing adaptation to shifting political, social, and economic contexts. Additionally, federalism's focus on managing diversity through regional autonomy can sometimes inadvertently reinforce regional identities, potentially stoking aspirations for complete independence among marginalized or underrepresented regional groups.

Fiscal inefficiency is another criticism of federal systems, where financial resource distribution can lead to uneven economic development and disparities in regional service delivery. This often results in inefficient national resource allocation and competition among states or regions. Coordinating national policies in federal systems is also challenging, given the diversity of regional policies in critical areas such as healthcare, environmental regulation, and immigration. This diversity can conflict with overarching national goals, complicating the formulation and implementation of cohesive national strategies.

In social policy, regional customization—while beneficial—can also contribute to disparities in education, healthcare, and welfare services. Such disparities can exacerbate social inequality, especially in nations with significant regional differences in standards of education and healthcare.

---

22 Birkland, 2008

Federal systems also encounter challenges in aligning national interests with global commitments in an increasingly interconnected world. Addressing issues that require unified national responses, such as climate change, international trade, and global health crises, becomes more complex in systems with substantial regional autonomy.

In summary, federalism, while dynamic and adaptable, confronts significant criticism and limitations. Its complexities and inefficiencies can affect crisis management, national policy coordination, and equitable service provision. Federal systems must navigate challenges in balancing national unity with regional diversity, aligning with global trends, and managing secessionist movements and ethnic conflicts. The efficacy and relevance of federal systems in today's interconnected world hinge on their ability to evolve and meet these challenges.

1.9. THE FUTURE OF FEDERALISM

Federalism is dynamically evolving in response to the rapidly changing global landscape characterized by technological advancements, political shifts, and evolving social dynamics. Looking ahead, we can expect significant transformations in federalism as it adapts to these emerging trends and challenges.

Innovations are likely to focus on enhancing the efficiency, transparency, and responsiveness of federal systems. A pivotal area of transformation is the integration of technology in governance. E-governance initiatives, harnessing the power of digital tools, are poised to streamline administrative processes, improve service delivery, and bolster citizen engagement. Digital platforms could revolutionize intergovernmental communication and facilitate real-time public participation in policy formulation[23].

Fiscal federalism is poised for innovation with the potential development of advanced revenue sharing and fiscal transfer mech-

---

23 Goldsmith and Georges, 2014

anisms that are responsive to changing economic conditions and regional needs. Employing data analytics and economic modeling could result in more dynamic and equitable fiscal policies, ensuring regions are well-equipped for their responsibilities[24].

Another domain ripe for reform is intergovernmental relations, where a focus on cooperative federalism may lead to joint task forces or committees comprising representatives from various government levels to tackle issues that transcend such jurisdictional boundaries as climate change, healthcare, and infrastructure development.

On a global scale, federalism must adapt to trends such as increasing emphasis on local governance and subsidiarity, potentially leading to more power and resources being devolved to local authorities within federal structures. This aligns with the global movement toward decentralization and community-driven development[25].

Balancing national sovereignty and global interconnectedness is another impending challenge. Federal systems will need to manage adeptly their roles in international agreements and entities such as the European Union. This necessitates reassessing the roles of federal and regional governments in international institutions and agreements and for advocating for more coordinated global engagement.

Federalism's future will also be shaped by addressing universal challenges like climate change, migration, and global health crises. Formulating flexible and innovative policies that are locally relevant and globally coherent will be vital. Collaboration among federal and regional governments, international organizations, NGOs, and the private sector will be key to developing comprehensive solutions.

The advent of digital technology and artificial intelligence presents both opportunities and challenges. While technological advancements can enhance governance effectiveness, they also bring concerns about privacy, security, and the digital divide. Federal

---

24 Boadway and Shah, 2009
25 Burgess, 2006

systems must adapt to these technological shifts, ensuring digital governance models are equitable and accessible to all citizens.

In conclusion, the future of federalism is likely to be characterized by innovation, adaptation, and reform. As the world becomes increasingly complex and interconnected, federal systems will need to evolve to address the challenges and opportunities of this new era. Advancements in technology, fiscal policy, and intergovernmental relations, combined with a nuanced approach to global challenges, will be crucial. The adaptability and resilience of federal systems will play a vital role in serving diverse populations while maintaining a coherent and unified governance structure.

CHAPTER 2

COMPARATIVE ANALYSIS OF FEDERALISM: GLOBAL PERSPECTIVES

2.1. INTRODUCTION

Federalism takes on various forms worldwide, each mirroring the distinctive sociopolitical and historical backdrop of its country. This comparative analysis endeavors to investigate these diverse models of federalism, focusing on how different nations distribute power between their central and regional governments. This chapter examines the ramifications of these power dynamics for broader governance, societal cohesion, and the process of national integration. Such an exploration reveals the intricate balance and trade-offs inherent in federal systems and how they shape the functioning of governments and societies.

Examining the well-established federal frameworks of countries like the United States and Germany and the developing federal structures in emerging economies and nations recovering from conflict, this analysis aims to uncover the complex and varied nature of federalism as it is practiced across the globe. It offers a window into how countries with mature federal systems have refined their governance over time and how newer federations are adapting this model to their unique circumstances. Through this examination, we gain a deeper understanding of the universal principles of federalism and of the nuanced ways in which these principles are applied, revealing the adaptability and global relevance of federal systems in addressing the contemporary challenges of governance and unity.

2.2. FEDERALISM IN ESTABLISHED DEMOCRACIES (UNITED STATES, CANADA, GERMANY)

Federalism serves as a foundational governance model that expertly balances regional diversity and local autonomy with national unity, showcasing its effectiveness particularly in established democracies like the United States, Germany, and Canada. Influenced by unique historical, cultural, and political factors, each of these nations has developed a distinct approach to federalism.

The approach to federalism in the United States was initially crafted to address the inefficiencies of the country's Articles of Confederation, which had left the young nation with a weak central government and overpowering state authorities. With the ratification of the US constitution in 1788, a more balanced approach was introduced that established a robust federal structure while affirming significant powers to the individual states. This created a system known as dual federalism, where state and federal governments operate independently within clearly delineated boundaries[26].

Over time, particularly beginning with the challenges of the Great Depression in the 1930s, the US federalism model transitioned toward a more cooperative form. This new phase, often referred to as cooperative federalism, encouraged a more collaborative approach between state and federal governments with shared responsibilities for addressing more complex societal issues. This model facilitated various national programs during the New Deal era, fostering a partnership that has evolved to address modern challenges such as environmental legislation, healthcare, and education reform[27].

Despite its evolution, the US federal system occasionally experiences tensions, especially in instances where state policies clash with federal mandates. These conflicts can lead to disparities in resource distribution and policy implementation, reflecting the ongoing struggle to balance state independence with federal oversight.

---

26 O'Toole, 1993
27 Peterson, 1995

However, the system's inherent flexibility has proved invaluable, particularly in times of crisis, such as during natural disasters and the recent COVID-19 pandemic, highlighting federalism's capacity to adapt and respond effectively.

Following World War II, Germany embraced a cooperative federalism model in stark contrast to its more centralized past. The Basic Law of 1949 established a federal system in which power is shared between the federal government and the Länder (states). This arrangement is characterized by a significant degree of interdependence and cooperation, especially in legislative processes. The Bundesrat, which represents the states, must approve all legislation affecting state interests, ensuring that regional perspectives are considered in national policy-making[28].

This cooperative stance is further reinforced by Germany's fiscal equalization scheme, which redistributes resources to reduce economic disparities across the states. Such mechanisms ensure a balance between regional autonomy and national consistency and are crucial for maintaining uniformity in policy implementation across diverse states. However, German federalism is not without its challenges; it must continuously adapt to the pressures of regionalist movements and the complexities of modern governance, including European integration and global economic pressures[29].

Canadian federalism, established under the British North America Act of 1867, uniquely integrates the principles of bilingualism and multiculturalism into its federal structure. This approach not only acknowledges the country's diverse population but also allows substantial powers to be devolved to the provinces. Provinces like Quebec, Newfoundland, and Labrador enjoy significant autonomy, particularly in managing healthcare, education, and natural resources, enabling them to tailor policies to their specific demographic and cultural needs[30]. Despite its strengths, Canadian fed-

---

28 Jeffery, 1999
29 Umbach, 2002
30 LaSelva, 1996

eralism faces challenges such as interprovincial trade barriers and the full integration of indigenous rights within the federal framework.

Fiscal federalism varies significantly across the three countries. In the United States, individual states enjoy considerable autonomy in managing their revenues and expenditures, yet they depend on substantial federal transfers to alleviate regional financial inequities[31]. Conversely, Canada employs a robust equalization payment system designed to harmonize the ability of all provinces to provide comparable public services, effectively minimizing fiscal disparities[32]. Germany, meanwhile, adopts a cooperative approach to fiscal federalism, where states have limited authority to set taxes and rely on a complex equalization scheme that aims to maintain consistent living standards throughout the country[33]. Each model reflects a distinct strategy for balancing regional autonomy with national unity, addressing specific economic and social challenges inherent in the country's federal structures.

Regarding judiciary systems, the United States operates a dual court system where the federal judiciary functions independently from the state courts. The US Supreme Court sits at the pinnacle, holding supreme authority to interpret the constitution and settle disputes between states and the federal government[34]. In contrast, Canada employs a more integrated judicial system. Provincial courts under the supervision of the federal government, and the Supreme Court of Canada as the ultimate appellate body, effectively merge federal and provincial legal issues within its jurisdiction[35]. Germany, on the other hand, implements a specialized judiciary structure with distinct federal courts that function alongside state courts, each with specific jurisdictions. Notably, the Federal Constitutional Court addresses constitutional issues, including those involving the Länder

---

31 Oates, 1999
32 Boadway and Shah, 2007
33 Benz and Broschek, 2013
34 Chemerinsky, 2023
35 Hogg, 1985

(states), thus reinforcing the principles of cooperative federalism within its judiciary system[36]. These diverse systems each demonstrate unique approaches to allocating judicial responsibilities, achieving a balance between national oversight and regional autonomy, and maintaining legal coherence while respecting local legal particularities.

The examination of federalism in the United States, Germany, and Canada reveals a dynamic range of approaches, each tailored to specific national and local conditions yet all aimed at harmonizing the diverse needs of their societies. From the blend of dual and cooperative federalism in the United States to Germany's integrated legislative system and Canada's focus on multicultural inclusivity, these models of federalism demonstrate the capacity of each system of governance to foster regional self-determination, ensure national cohesion, and adapt to the cultural diversity of complex, modern societies. These cases provide valuable lessons in the delicate art of balancing central authority with regional autonomy, illustrating federalism's adaptability and enduring relevance.

2.3. FEDERALISM IN MULTINATIONAL STATES (INDIA, SWITZERLAND, BELGIUM)

Federalism serves as a crucial governance framework in multinational states, adeptly managing diversity while fostering national unity. This is particularly evident in India, Switzerland, and Belgium, where federal systems are uniquely customized to accommodate the complex realities of societies marked by diverse linguistic, cultural, and ethnic backgrounds. Each country's approach to federalism reflects its specific circumstances and challenges, demonstrating the system's adaptability and effectiveness in promoting cohesion and regional autonomy.

In India, federalism was adopted with the country's independence in 1947 in recognition of the nation's vast linguistic, cultural,

---

36 Jakob, Dyevre, and Itzcovich, 2017

and ethnic diversity. The Indian constitution, ratified in 1950, introduced a quasi-federal system with a central tilt that ensures a tripartite division of legislative powers into union, state, and concurrent lists. This structure allows for a balance of power that supports unity while accommodating the country's diversity. The reorganization of states along linguistic lines in the 1950s was a significant step in aligning state boundaries with cultural and linguistic identities, enhancing administrative efficiency, and strengthening regional identities. Despite ongoing challenges such as regional disparities and ethnic tensions, India's federal system has shown flexibility, adapting over time to accommodate new states and evolving demands for autonomy[37].

Switzerland's federalism, established following the Sonderbund War in 1848, is characterized by consociational federalism blended with direct democracy, where significant autonomy is granted to the cantons. This allows for local management of sectors like education and healthcare, ensuring that policies are tailored to local cultural and linguistic contexts. Swiss federalism also features a strong component of direct democracy, where citizens can initiate constitutional amendments and challenge laws through referendums; this promotes inclusivity and public participation at all levels of government. This model has been effective in managing the country's linguistic and cultural diversity through a sophisticated fiscal federalism system that ensures equitable distribution of financial resources among the cantons[38].

Belgium's federal system evolved from a unitary state to a federal state in response to deep-seated linguistic and cultural divisions between the Flemish and Walloon populations. The Belgian federal structure now includes distinct regions and communities that have significant autonomy over areas like education and culture, while the federal government handles broader national and international issues. This division of powers has been instrumental in reducing tensions and fostering stability, although challenges, including

---

37 Riker, 1964
38 Linder, 1994

economic disparities and governance complexities, remain due to consensual politics[39].

In India, the fiscal structure is centralized, with specific revenue-sharing mechanisms defined by the Constitution. The central government collects the majority of tax revenues and redistributes them among the states through the Finance Commission to ensure equitable distribution and minimize regional economic disparities[40]. In stark contrast, Switzerland boasts highly autonomous cantons and municipalities that independently manage their fiscal affairs, including taxation and expenditures. Switzerland employs a sophisticated equalization mechanism, which includes resource equalization and cost compensation aimed at reducing fiscal imbalances among cantons and promoting economic development evenly across the country[41]. Meanwhile, Belgium has undergone significant fiscal decentralization since the 1980s, granting increased fiscal autonomy to its regions and communities. This decentralization has facilitated more localized policy-making but has also ignited fiscal competition among the regions, posing challenges in balancing regional autonomy with national cohesion[42].

The judicial systems in India, Switzerland, and Belgium each reflect the influence of their respective federal structures. India features an integrated judiciary where a single hierarchical system administers both central and state laws, with the Supreme Court at its apex overseeing a broad spectrum of national issues. This system is designed to maintain a uniform application of law across the diverse states, ensuring consistency and fairness in judicial processes[43]. Switzerland operates a dual judiciary system; its Federal Supreme Court in Lausanne ensures the uniform application of federal law across all cantons, while cantonal courts manage local civil and criminal cases;

---

39 Swenden, 2006
40 Rao and Singh, 2006
41 Dafflon, 2002
42 Deschouwer, 2009
43 Sathe, 2003

this arrangement epitomizes the nation's commitment to combining local judicial autonomy with federal oversight[44]. In Belgium, the judicial system is deeply entwined with the country's complex federal structure and linguistic divisions. These divisions significantly affect judicial operations, from the appointment of judges to court administration, integrating regional and community interests into the national judicial framework, and underscoring Belgium's unique approach to accommodating linguistic diversity within its federal system[45]. Each system illustrates different methods of distributing judicial authority, ensuring both accessibility and consistency in legal proceedings.

The experiences of India, Switzerland, and Belgium with federalism offer profound insights into how this governance model can effectively manage diversity within a nation. Each system is thoughtfully crafted to address specific regional, cultural, and linguistic needs, illustrating the flexibility and dynamic nature of federalism. India's approach has been critical in managing its diverse array of languages and ethnicities, Switzerland's model emphasizes local autonomy and direct democracy, and Belgium's system focuses on balancing linguistic and regional divides.

These varied implementations of federalism demonstrate its capacity to foster national cohesion and regional self-determination, making it a valuable model for other countries with similar diversity challenges. The success of these federal systems in adapting to changing societal needs and maintaining unity amid deep diversity provides valuable lessons for nations worldwide. As these countries continue to evolve, their experiences remain relevant, underscoring the effectiveness of federal structures in harmonizing a nation's multifaceted identity.

---

44 Fleiner-Gerster, Misic, and Töpperwien, 2005
45 Reuchamps, 2015

2.4. FEDERALISM IN EMERGING ECONOMIES (BRAZIL, NIGERIA, RUSSIA)

Federalism in emerging economies provides a distinctive perspective characterized by rapid economic growth, regional disparities, and varied sociopolitical complexities. This exploration into nations like Brazil, Nigeria, and Russia offers insights into how federal systems function amid the dynamic evolution of these growing economies. Each country employs federalism in a unique way to manage economic development, ethnic diversity, and political centralization, reflecting its individual needs and challenges.

Brazil's federalism has evolved significantly since its independence in 1822 and has developed into a complex system articulated in the 1988 "Citizen Constitution." This constitution formalizes the division of powers among the union, twenty-six states, the federal district, and more than 5,500 municipalities. It grants states autonomy over areas such as education and health while reserving areas such as national defense and foreign policy to the federal government. Brazilian federalism, characterized by both cooperative and competitive elements, varies widely in socioeconomic development across states, with wealthier states like São Paulo and Rio de Janeiro contrasting sharply with less developed areas. A key aspect of Brazil's federalism is its approach to environmental governance, especially in managing the Amazon rainforest, and to the balance of local, national, and global interests. Fiscal federalism plays a crucial role, involving complex revenue distribution and fiscal responsibilities, which, while intended to address economic disparities, have led to disputes and challenges in fiscal management. Political instability and corruption have occasionally strained federal–state relations, impacting governance efficacy. Despite these challenges, Brazilian federalism remains critical for accommodating regional diversity and promoting democratic governance, enabling region-specific policies to address the diverse needs of its population[46].

---

46 Samuels, 2003

In Nigeria, federalism was adopted as a governance strategy to manage the country's profound ethnic diversity and complex sociopolitical landscape following the country's independence in 1960. With more than 250 ethnic groups, federalism has been central in balancing national unity with ethnic aspirations. Nigerian federalism evolved from the colonial amalgamation of different regions to the formal adoption of a federal structure in 1963 to balance power among its diverse regions. This system, however, exacerbated ethnic and regional disparities, contributing to political instability and conflict, notably to the civil war known as the Biafran War. The subsequent expansion to thirty-six states was aimed at reducing ethnic tensions and fostering national integration. Nigerian federalism features a strong central government with a defined power separation across different governmental levels, but it also wrestles with the contentious issue of resource control, particularly the control of oil in the Niger Delta. The derivation principle, intended to equitably distribute oil revenues, has been a focal point of debate regarding fiscal federalism and equity. Ethnic and religious conflicts remain a significant challenge, necessitating a delicate balance between regional autonomy and national unity[47].

Russia's federal system reflects the country's vast geography, ethnic diversity, and the historical shifts following the Soviet Union's collapse. Initially implicit during the Tsarist era and later more structured under Soviet centralization, Russian federalism was transformed with the 1991 dissolution of the Soviet Union, creating a federation of eighty-nine federal subjects. Under President Yeltsin, the 1990s marked a period of significant decentralization that granted substantial autonomy to regional entities. However, Vladimir Putin's presidency has shifted the country toward centralization, aligning regional policies with federal laws and centralizing political power. Economically, Russia faces regional disparities with uneven distribution of natural resources, a challenge for federal governance that aims to balance economic equity across regions. Politically, Russian feder-

---

[47] Mustapha and Whitfield, 2009

alism strives to reconcile national cohesion with ethnic and regional diversity, navigating the complexities of a centralized approach that emphasizes a unified Russian identity while acknowledging regional distinctiveness[48].

Fiscally, the Brazilian constitution delineates a multi-tiered fiscal system where states and municipalities have significant autonomy in collecting certain taxes, while the federal government retains control over key revenue streams, redistributing them through transfer mechanisms to ensure equitable financial allocation across diverse regions. This complex arrangement is critical in addressing the country's vast socioeconomic disparities[49]. Nigeria's fiscal federalism is heavily influenced by its oil revenue, with the federal government controlling the majority of these resources and distributing them to states through a statutory allocation formula. This system aims to balance the wealth generated from oil-rich regions with the needs of less endowed areas, although it has often led to tensions and calls for greater fiscal autonomy at the state level[50]. In contrast, Russia's fiscal federalism has evolved from a highly centralized system under the Soviet Union to one that, post-1991, gave considerable revenue-generating powers to its regions. More recently, under Putin's administration, there has been a significant recentralization, with the federal government reclaiming control over key financial resources and reducing the fiscal independence of the regions[51].

The judiciary systems in Brazil, Nigeria, and Russia reflect their federal structures but face unique challenges related to the enforcement of federal principles. Brazil's judiciary is characterized by a strong federal court system with the Supreme Federal Court at its apex to ensure uniform interpretation of constitutional law across the country. This system plays a crucial role in mediating disputes between state and federal laws, contributing to a coherent legal

---

48 Stoner-Weiss, 2006
49 Arretche, 2019
50 Suberu, 2001
51 Zhuravskaya, 2000

framework nationwide[52]. Nigeria's judiciary, while formally structured to balance powers between federal and state authorities, often struggles with enforcement issues and corruption, which undermine its effectiveness. The Nigerian federal government's control over the appointment of judges to the Supreme Court can also influence how federalism is implemented and perceived at the state level[53]. In Russia, the judicial system has undergone significant reforms since the dissolution of the Soviet Union, with the introduction of a constitutional court that plays a key role in interpreting federal laws and mediates between the federal center and the regions. However, the judiciary is often criticized for lacking independence from the federal government, which impacts its role in sustaining a genuine federal structure[54].

The exploration of federalism in Brazil, Nigeria, and Russia presents a compelling study of how this governance model functions within the unique contexts of emerging economies. These nations demonstrate the intricate balance federalism strives to maintain between regional diversity, resource distribution, and national unity. Each country's approach highlights the challenges and opportunities inherent in adapting federal systems to local realities. Brazil showcases how federalism can facilitate local governance while grappling with economic and political disparities. Nigeria illustrates the complexities of managing a resource-rich, ethnically diverse nation under a federal system. Russia offers insights into the dynamics between centralization and decentralization in a vast, resource-endowed country. Collectively, these examples underscore the necessity for federal systems to continually evolve and respond to changing socioeconomic, political, and environmental conditions, providing valuable lessons for other nations with similar complexities.

---

52 Taylor, 2008
53 Suberu, 2001
54 Solomon, 2004

2.5. FEDERALISM IN POST-CONFLICT SOCIETIES (BOSNIA, HERZEGOVINA, ETHIOPIA, IRAQ)

Federalism has often been applied in post-conflict societies to mitigate deep-seated ethnic, religious, and regional divisions. By decentralizing power and recognizing the rights of diverse groups, federal systems aim to promote peace, stability, and reconciliation in communities fragmented by conflict. Notable examples include Bosnia and Herzegovina, Ethiopia, and Iraq, each demonstrating distinct challenges and outcomes of federalism in post-conflict environments.

In Bosnia and Herzegovina, the federal system was established by the Dayton Peace Accords that ended the Bosnian War in 1995. This complex model divided the country into two autonomous entities: the Federation of Bosnia and Herzegovina, mainly inhabited by Bosniaks and Croats, and the Republika Srpska, which is predominantly Serbian; the Brčko District was established within the Federation of Bosnia and Herzegovina as a neutral, self-governing unit. Each entity has considerable autonomy, including its own president, government, parliament, and police force. The central government in Sarajevo handles national matters like defense and foreign policy, though its powers are limited. The presidency rotates among representatives of the three main ethnic groups. This structure has maintained peace but is often criticized for perpetuating ethnic divisions and causing governance inefficiencies, including overlapping responsibilities and the necessity for ethnic group consensus, which often leads to bureaucratic and political impasses[55].

Ethiopia's approach to ethnic federalism was established following the overthrow of the Derg regime in 1991. The 1995 Constitution divided the country into regions or states based largely on ethnic lines, granting them the right to choose official languages and to control local government, police, and education. The federal government retained authority over defense, foreign affairs, and

---

55 Chandler, 2000

major fiscal and economic policies. This structure has empowered ethnic groups, particularly those historically marginalized, but has also heightened ethnic tensions, sometimes leading to violence. The central challenge of Ethiopian federalism is balancing self-determination with national unity, particularly as the focus on ethnic identity has sometimes deepened divisions rather than fostered integration[56].

Iraq's federal system, which emerged after the US-led 2003 invasion and the fall of Saddam Hussein's regime, was designed to accommodate the country's complex ethnic, religious, and regional dynamics. The 2005 Iraqi constitution established federalism that offers autonomy to various groups, notably the Kurds in the north, while aiming to maintain state integrity. Iraqi federalism includes a central government responsible for defense, foreign affairs, and fiscal policy, with regional autonomy for areas like Kurdistan, which has its own government, parliament, and security forces. This system was intended to manage sectarian and ethnic divisions among Shiites, Sunnis, and Kurds and to prevent conflict through power distribution. However, tensions have persisted, especially concerning oil and revenue sharing between the central government and regions like Kurdistan[57].

In Bosnia and Herzegovina, fiscal federalism is highly complex, characterized by a fragmented system that mirrors the country's intricate political structure. Each entity—the Federation of Bosnia and Herzegovina and the Republika Srpska—manages its own budget, with minimal fiscal coordination between the two; this leads to inefficiencies and regional disparities. This has significantly impacted the country's overall economic stability and development[58]. Ethiopia's approach to fiscal federalism involves significant decentralization. This allows its ethnically based regions to retain substantial revenue from local taxes while the federal government redistributes the main revenue streams to ensure equitable develop-

---

56 Turton, 2006
57 Galbraith, 2007
58 Bose, 2002

ment across regions. This system aims to balance regional autonomy with national cohesion but has faced challenges in implementation and has often exacerbated regional inequalities[59]. In contrast, Iraq's fiscal federalism is heavily centralized, with the federal government controlling the vast majority of oil revenue that constitutes the bulk of the country's wealth. However, the Kurdistan region has negotiated terms that grant it a degree of fiscal autonomy, including a share of oil revenues, which have been a continuous source of tension with the central government[60].

The judiciary systems in Bosnia and Herzegovina, Ethiopia, and Iraq also reflect the federal dynamics of each state, although each faces various challenges. In Bosnia and Herzegovina, a complex judicial system aligns with its federal structure. This system has entity-level courts and a constitutional court that deals with disputes between state levels and interprets the constitution. This system, however, is often criticized for its inefficiency and susceptibility to political interference[61]. Ethiopia's judiciary is theoretically designed to allow ethnic regions to apply federal laws contextually while maintaining the uniform application of constitutional principles across the state. Nevertheless, the judiciary's capacity to act independently has been questioned, with concerns about its ability to mediate conflicts impartially between the federal center and the regions[62]. Iraq's judiciary, reformed post-2003, includes federal courts intended to oversee federal matters and to mediate disputes between Baghdad and the regions, particularly the Kurdistan regional government. However, political instability and ongoing conflict significantly challenge the judiciary's effectiveness and its role in upholding federal principles[63].

These case studies illustrate that while federalism can be a valuable strategy in post-conflict scenarios to accommodate diverse

---

59 Fessha, 2010
60 O'Leary, 2009
61 Perry, 2009
62 Abbink, 2006
63 Dawisha, 2009

group interests and foster peace, it also carries the risk of entrenching the divisions it aims to resolve. In Bosnia and Herzegovina, the federal arrangement has been criticized for reinforcing ethnic separations. In Ethiopia, while providing a degree of self-determination, federalism has sometimes aggravated ethnic tensions. In Iraq, despite helping to manage diversity, federalism struggles with integrating various groups and managing resource-related conflicts. These examples highlight the success of federalism in post-conflict societies as depending on careful structuring and implementation that is tailored to the specific historical, cultural, and sociopolitical context of each nation. The balance between granting autonomy to various groups and fostering a unified national identity is crucial, as is the role of external actors, in shaping the federal system's trajectory.

2.6. COMPARATIVE ANALYSIS OF FISCAL FEDERALISM

Fiscal federalism, a critical aspect of federal systems, involves the distribution of financial resources and fiscal responsibilities among different government levels. Its management significantly impacts economic equality, efficiency, and regional development. A comparison of various federal systems offers insights into handling the challenges and opportunities presented by this form of federalism. This analysis examines revenue sharing and the dimensions of fiscal autonomy across different federal frameworks, emphasizing their role in fostering economic equality and regional growth.

2.6.1 Revenue Sharing and Fiscal Autonomy in Diverse Federal Systems

The concept of revenue sharing and fiscal autonomy within diverse federal systems plays a pivotal role in shaping economic equality and maintaining a balance between regional autonomy and national governance. This balancing act varies significantly across different countries, influenced by each nation's unique historical, political, and economic contexts. Understanding how these systems operate can provide critical insights into the complexities and nuances of fiscal federalism, which in turn affect broader aspects of governance and public policy.

In the United States, the federal system grants substantial fiscal independence to the states, allowing them to create and manage their own tax systems and budgetary spending. This decentralization is crucial for tailoring fiscal policies to local needs, fostering a sense of innovation and adaptability. However, this autonomy also comes with challenges, particularly in terms of disparities in the provision of public services across different states. While some states, benefiting from robust economies, can fund comprehensive services, others with less fiscal capacity struggle to meet basic needs. Federal grants-in-aid play a significant role in this context, aiming to level the playing field somewhat by providing targeted funds for specific state programs. Despite these efforts, achieving a truly equitable distribution of resources remains a challenge, highlighting a fundamental tension within the US federal system between state flexibility and the need for national fiscal coherence.

Germany presents a stark contrast with its more centralized approach to fiscal federalism. Both federal and state governments have the authority to levy taxes, but a significant portion of these funds is redistributed through an equalization system. This system is designed to ensure that all regions of Germany maintain a uniform standard of living, thus promoting a sense of equity across the federation. The aim is to achieve service equivalence throughout the country, though this can sometimes suppress regional fiscal initiatives and potentially stifle local innovation due to a perceived lack of fiscal autonomy. Nevertheless, this approach prioritizes national coherence over regional flexibility, reflecting a different set of priorities in governance.

Canada's fiscal federalism represents a middle ground between the decentralized American model and Germany's centralized system. The Canadian system features both shared and exclusive revenue sources for the federal and provincial governments, with federal equalization payments designed to reduce fiscal disparities across provinces. This arrangement reflects Canada's commitment to balancing provincial autonomy with the necessity of maintaining national fiscal equity as it strives to ensure that all regions can provide comparable levels of public services while also respecting the unique economic and fiscal capacities of each province.

In Nigeria, the focus of fiscal federalism is predominantly on the equitable distribution of oil revenues, which are central to the nation's economy. The derivation principle, which allocates oil revenues to the states where the oil is produced, is intended to balance regional interests and foster local economic development. However, this has led to considerable conflict and tension as regions that do not produce oil often feel marginalized or unfairly treated. This situation highlights the challenges of managing natural resources in a federal system, where the equitable distribution of wealth is crucial for national stability and cohesion.

Switzerland showcases a model that emphasizes cantonal fiscal autonomy, where significant fiscal policies are managed by the cantons themselves. These are balanced by national fiscal equalization mechanisms to ensure that resources are fairly distributed. This model supports regional diversity and allows for tailored fiscal policies that suit local conditions, while still maintaining a cohesive national framework. Switzerland's approach exemplifies how a nation can foster regional autonomy within a robust national system, ensuring that local governance can adapt to specific regional needs without compromising national unity.

Each of these federal systems—from the United States to Switzerland—demonstrates different approaches to managing the intricate balance between local demands and national policies. The diversity of these systems provides valuable lessons for countries looking to evolve or reform their federal structures, highlighting the necessity for adapting to specific socioeconomic and cultural realities. Balancing regional autonomy with national fiscal responsibilities is key to ensuring equitable development and respecting the integrity of local governance.

2.6.2 Fiscal Federalism's Role in Economic Equality and Regional Development

The structure of fiscal federalism significantly shapes the capabilities of regional governments to provide essential services and stimulate economic growth, directly influencing economic equality and regional development. This system of financial governance can markedly affect how regions flourish or falter based on the balance struck between centralized and decentralized fiscal control.

Germany's approach to fiscal federalism is particularly illustrative of a centralized system designed to mitigate economic disparities across its federal states. Wealthier states like Bavaria, with their robust industrial bases, contrast sharply with economically weaker states such as Brandenburg. Through mechanisms like equalization payments and shared tax revenues, Germany redistributes wealth to enhance public services and infrastructure in its less prosperous regions. This redistribution not only helps level the playing field but also fosters more uniform regional development, aiming to ensure that all citizens have access to a comparable quality of life regardless of their state's economic wealth.

Conversely, in the United States, the model of fiscal federalism grants substantial autonomy to individual states, empowering them to formulate and implement their own economic policies. This degree of freedom enables states like California and Texas to innovate and compete economically on a national and international scale. However, this same autonomy also creates significant disparities among the states, as regions like Mississippi and New Mexico might struggle to marshal the necessary resources to match the public services and infrastructure projects of their more affluent counterparts. This disparity can lead to a patchwork of economic prosperity and challenge, highlighting the double-edged sword of decentralized fiscal governance.

Canada's fiscal federalism embodies a hybrid approach, incorporating elements of both centralized and decentralized models. The federal government uses transfers, including equalization payments, to smooth out fiscal disparities between richer provinces like Alberta and poorer ones like New Brunswick. This system strives to maintain a balance between respecting provincial autonomy and ensuring a degree of national economic uniformity, thus supporting a cohesive national economy while allowing provincial differences to flourish.

In Nigeria, fiscal federalism is crucial for the distribution of oil revenues, which significantly impact the country's economic landscape. The derivation principle seeks to distribute oil revenues fairly among the producing states to foster regional economic development. However, this focus on resource allocation has led to economic dependencies and stark development disparities, as regions not enriched by oil resources often lag behind in infrastructure and public services, creating regional economic imbalances.

Brazil's model of fiscal federalism allows considerable autonomy to its states and municipalities. This autonomy enables economically vibrant regions like São Paulo to excel and innovate, driving national economic growth. However, it also results in fiscal imbalances where poorer states struggle to fund adequate public services, leading to uneven regional development and challenges in national cohesion.

The balance between centralization and decentralization in fiscal federalism is thus crucial. While decentralized systems like those in the United States and Brazil promote regional policy innovation and economic dynamism, they also risk creating significant disparities. Centralized systems, such as those in Germany and Canada, help support uniform development but must be careful not to overly constrain the autonomy that can drive regional initiative and adaptation.

In conclusion, the role of fiscal federalism in fostering economic equality and regional development is multifaceted and varies significantly across the world. Each system's effectiveness hinges on its ability to adapt to regional needs while maintaining a commitment to national economic stability and equity. This adaptability is key to ensuring that fiscal federalism effectively contributes to both regional prosperity and national coherence.

2.7. GOVERNANCE AND POLITICAL PARTICIPATION IN FEDERAL SYSTEMS

Federal systems provide a distinctive platform for governance and political participation and are characterized by intricate interactions between multiple levels of government and a wide array of participants. These systems profoundly influence democracy and political engagement by structuring governance in a way that enhances citizen involvement. The roles of political parties and civil society are critical in maximizing the effectiveness of federal systems and contribute to a more engaged and responsive political landscape[64].

At its core, federalism promotes deeper democratic engagement and political participation by distributing power across various state, provincial, and regional governments. This decentralization not only facilitates a more direct connection between governments and citizens but also enhances the representation of diverse populations, making political involvement more accessible. For instance, in India, state governments address the specific needs of their constituents; this reflects the country's vast diversity in language, culture, and socioeconomic conditions and leads to tailored governance approaches that resonate more closely with local concerns and encourage higher participation rates in regional governance processes. Similarly, in the United States, state and local governments, because of their proximity to the citizenry, often deal with issues that affect daily life directly, which tends to increase civic engagement and voter turnout[65].

Federal systems inherently support political pluralism, which is vital for the health of democracies. By allowing multiple voices to be heard and enabling various groups to have a say in the political process, federal systems prevent the concentration of power and

---

64 Elazar, 1987
65 Elazar, 1984

encourage a diverse range of opinions and debates. The Swiss federal model exemplifies this, granting significant autonomy to cantons and thereby ensuring that the unique interests of different linguistic and cultural communities are protected and represented. This not only preserves national unity but also enriches the democratic process by incorporating regional diversity into national policy-making[66].

However, federal systems are not without their challenges. One major issue is the confusion that can arise among citizens concerning which level of government is responsible for specific services; this confusion can lead to political disengagement. Additionally, the task of balancing power between different levels of government can be complex and delicate. In Nigeria, for example, federalism is employed to manage the country's profound ethnic diversity. Yet achieving a harmonious balance of power that satisfies all constituents continually remains a challenge[67].

Political parties play a crucial dual role in federal systems. Operating across both national and regional levels they are able to address a broad spectrum of interests, from local to national, enhancing policy coordination and ensuring that diverse regional interests are considered in national discourse. In Canada and Germany, political parties effectively bridge the gap between different levels of government, promoting the policy coherence and continuity that are essential for effective governance[68].

Civil society also plays a fundamental role in federal systems. Non-governmental organizations, special-interest groups, and community organizations advocate for a range of issues including the rights and needs of minorities and marginalized communities. These entities engage in policy advocacy, monitor government performance, and raise public awareness, thereby fostering more transparent and accountable governance. In Brazil, for example, civil society movements have played a crucial role in elevating environ-

---

66 Linder, 1994
67 Suberu, 2001
68 Detterbeck, 2005

mental and social issues to the national stage, thereby influencing policy and public opinion[69].

Overall, federalism significantly impacts governance and political participation by providing a structured yet flexible framework that enhances democratic engagement and ensures diverse representation. This system not only facilitates closer interactions between the government and its citizens but it also supports a rich tapestry of political pluralism. However, meticulous management is required to avoid the complexities that could undermine effective governance. The roles of political parties and civil society are indispensable in this framework because they enrich the democratic process and ensure that governance is effective, inclusive, and reflective of the populace's diverse needs.

As federal systems continue to evolve, the sustained integration of these entities in the decision-making process and their active participation are crucial. Their continued engagement highlights the need for a comprehensive approach to governance that addresses the intricate challenges inherent in federal systems. They ensure that governance remains responsive, inclusive, and effectively attuned to the diverse needs of the population. This approach is essential for maintaining a robust and dynamic federal system that can adapt to changing conditions and continue to serve the best interests of all citizens.

2.8. FEDERALISM AND SOCIAL POLICY

Federalism significantly influences the development and execution of social policies, particularly in healthcare, education, and welfare. Within this model of governance, the division of responsibilities between national and regional governments offers unique possibilities and challenges for catering to diverse population needs. This section analyzes the management of health, education, and welfare

---

[69] Hochstetler, 2000

policies within federal structures and discusses the role of regional governments in mitigating social inequality.

2.8.1 Management of Social Policies in Federal Systems

Federal systems around the world navigate the complex task of managing social policies, attempting to balance national standards with regional specificities. This governance structure often leads to a variety of policy approaches, each reflecting a country's unique sociopolitical nuances.

In healthcare, federal countries exhibit significant variations. For instance, Canada's healthcare system is managed predominantly by the provinces within federal guidelines, allowing for regional tailoring of healthcare services[70]. However, this approach can result in disparities in service quality across provinces. In contrast, Germany's more centralized healthcare system involves both federal and state governments and aims for consistent health standards nationwide. The German model emphasizes equitable access to healthcare for all citizens, regardless of their state of residence[71].

Education policy management also varies across federal systems. In the United States, education is primarily under state and local control, leading to a wide range of educational standards and funding[72]. This decentralization fosters local innovation but can also exacerbate disparities. In Australia, on the other hand, both federal and state governments play significant roles in education, with national-level funding and standards helping to mitigate regional differences and maintain a consistent quality of education across the country[73].

Welfare management in federal systems typically involves multiple layers of government. Brazil exemplifies this with federal, state, and municipal roles in social welfare, which necessitate strong

---

70 Marchildon and Allin, 2021
71 Busse and Blümel, 2014
72 Peterson, 2010
73 Connell, 2007

intergovernmental cooperation to achieve efficiency and uniformity in service delivery[74]. Conversely, Nigeria faces unique challenges in welfare management due to its diverse ethnic and regional composition. The Nigerian federal government sets broad welfare policies, but implementation often varies significantly at the state level where it is influenced by local economic conditions, cultural norms, and administrative capacities[75]. This results in varied welfare outcomes across different states, reflecting the complex interplay between federal directives and regional realities.

Managing social policies in federal systems is a balancing act between maintaining uniform national standards and accommodating regional particularities. Centralized models, like Germany's, focus on nationwide uniformity, while decentralized approaches, as seen in the United States, allow for regional innovation but risk creating disparities. Countries like Nigeria and Brazil illustrate the added complexities in multi-ethnic and economically diverse nations. The continuous evolution of these systems is crucial in ensuring equitable access to vital services, reflecting a persistent endeavor to harmonize regional diversity with national cohesion.

2.8.2 Regional Governments and Social Inequality

In federal systems, the role of regional governments is pivotal in addressing and mitigating social inequality. The proximity of regional governments to local communities places them in an advantageous position to understand and respond effectively to specific regional challenges related to poverty, health, and education. Regional governments can implement focused strategies to tackle issues like poverty, unemployment, and social exclusion. In India, for example, state governments often initiate programs aimed at alleviating poverty, improving healthcare, and enhancing educational opportunities in underdeveloped areas[76]. These targeted measures

---

74 Arretche, 2012
75 Suberu, 2001
76 Panagariya, Chakraborty, and Rao, 2014

ensure efficient resource allocation and address the unique needs of the local population.

In Brazil, regional initiatives play a significant role in addressing social inequalities within the country's diverse federal structure. States in Brazil have developed various social programs tailored to their demographic and socioeconomic contexts, addressing issues such as income inequality and access to basic services[77]. Regional governments in federal systems can also function as laboratories for innovation in social policy. They have the flexibility to experiment with new welfare models, healthcare reforms, and educational techniques. Successful regional initiatives can serve as models for adoption in other regions or at the national level. For example, Canada's provincial governments have pioneered various healthcare initiatives, some of which have influenced national healthcare policies[78].

Despite their strategic position, the ability of regional governments to combat social inequality is often contingent on their financial resources. Disparities in wealth and resource allocation among regions in a federal country can lead to uneven capacities to provide essential services. In the United States, for instance, there is significant variation between wealthier and poorer states in the quality and availability of social services, reflecting the impact of economic disparities on social policy management[79].

To mitigate these disparities, federal systems may employ fiscal transfers or equalization payments to ensure a basic standard of services across the country. Australia's system of fiscal equalization, for instance, aims to provide states and territories with the financial capacity to offer comparable levels of public services, thereby addressing regional socioeconomic disparities.

The effective management of social inequality in federal systems relies on the proactive and innovative approaches of regional gov-

---

77 Falleti, 2010
78 Marchildon and Allin, 2021
79 Peterson, 1995

ernments. While these governments are well placed to address local issues, their success is often contingent upon adequate fiscal resources and support from the national government. Balancing regional autonomy with national standards and ensuring equitable resource distribution remains a fundamental challenge in harnessing the full potential of regional governments in federal systems.

CHAPTER 3

FEDERALISM IN POST-CONFLICT AFRICAN CONTEXTS: A PATH TO PEACE AND STABILITY

3.1. INTRODUCTION

The concept of federalism is emerging as an increasingly viable strategy for addressing the complexities of post-conflict situations in Africa. In a continent marked by its vibrant ethnic, cultural, and linguistic diversity, African nations frequently encounter formidable challenges in rebuilding and unifying their societies following periods of conflict. This chapter delves into the application of federalism within these distinctive African contexts and critically examines its effectiveness in nurturing peace, enhancing political stability, and driving socioeconomic growth.

This exploration encompasses a variety of African countries that have transitioned to federal structures in the aftermath of conflict. By providing a comprehensive analysis of these nations, this chapter offers valuable insights into the efficacy of federalism as a governance model in these unique environments. It highlights the successes achieved, identifies the challenges faced, and extracts crucial lessons from the experiences of these nations. This nuanced understanding of federalism in the setting of post-conflict Africa serves as a lens through which the potential and limitations of this governance system can be better appreciated and understood.

3.2. HISTORICAL CONTEXT OF POST-CONFLICT SITUATIONS IN AFRICA

The post-colonial period in Africa has been characterized by a complex web of conflicts that include civil wars and inter-state disputes, predominantly stemming from the vestiges of colonial rule. The imposition of arbitrary borders by colonial powers, often neglecting the continent's intricate ethnic and cultural tapestry, significantly contributed to these conflicts. Post-independence, many African nations have faced challenges in fostering national identity, effective governance, and addressing socioeconomic issues. Notable conflicts include the Nigerian Civil War (1967–1970), also known as the Biafran War, which was driven in part by ethnic tensions and resource-control disputes[80]. The Rwandan Genocide of 1994, a devastating outcome of deep-rooted ethnic divisions accentuated by colonial legacies, resulted in the loss of around 800,000 lives[81]. The protracted Sudanese Civil Wars (1955–1972, 1983–2005) were fueled by religious, ethnic, and economic disparities[82]. These and numerous other conflicts highlight the complex array of challenges confronting post-colonial African states.

Ethnicity, a dominant social factor in Africa with its diverse tribes and languages, plays a critical role and has been a focal point of conflict. Colonial powers often employed "divide-and-rule" strategies, deepening ethnic divisions and leaving behind a legacy of distrust and rivalry. Culturally, Africa's rich diversity sometimes clashed with efforts to forge cohesive nation-states from diverse groups. Imposed national identities often conflicted with established cultural and tribal affiliations, resulting in resistance and, in some cases, armed conflict[83].

The transition from colonial rule to self-governance was frequently fraught with difficulty. A lack of democratic institutions and governance experience led to power struggles that often descended into authoritarianism or military dictatorships, further destabilizing these nascent nations[84].

---

80 Jorre, 1972
81 Prunier, 1997
82 Johnson, 2003
83 Lemarchand, 1972
84 Chabal and Daloz, 1999

Colonialism's enduring impact on modern African states is profound. The creation of arbitrary borders and the establishment of extractive economic systems by colonial powers left many post-colonial governments with frail economies and infrastructure. Indirect rule and ethnic favoritism during colonialism have perpetuated deep divisions that continue to influence inter-ethnic relations in numerous African countries[85]. Moreover, the colonial legacy through language, legal systems, and governance structures continues to shape the identities and operations of African states. While elements such as the introduction of modern education and legal systems have been beneficial, the disruption of traditional governance and economic systems has had far-reaching adverse effects. Post-colonial decolonization often resulted in a leadership vacuum, with newly independent states struggling to establish stable governance systems. Coupled with underdeveloped economies and lingering ethnic and cultural divides, these factors set the stage for many of the conflicts that have since unfolded in Africa[86].

3.3. EVOLUTION OF FEDERALISM IN AFRICA

Most of the countries in Africa gained independence from European colonial rule between 1950 and 1975 in what is regarded as the decolonization era of Africa[87]. Seventeen countries in the continent became independent nations and joined the United Nations in 1960, the year later known as The Year of Africa.

From day one after independence, the new African nations faced complex and long-neglected territorial, ethnic, sociopolitical, economic, and institutional challenges. These included weak institutional capacity, inexperienced leadership, and underdevelopment. They also included a lack of infrastructure, technical knowledge, and capacity for manufacturing as well as low levels of education. Ethnic fragmentation and pluralism created in part by the artificial bound-

---

85 Mamdani, 2018
86 Cooper, 2002
87 Birmingham, 1995

aries that cut across ethnic groups in the continent created further challenges.

Most of these new African nations grappled with the legacy models of statehood left behind by the colonial powers, with post-independence African leaders, most of them inexperienced, vying to occupy the seats of their colonial masters[88]. The new leaders were overwhelmed by the enormous tasks of maintaining peace, unity, harmony, social cohesion, national identity, and territorial integrity in the face of ethnic, cultural, and religious, and geopolitical diversity. In response to these challenges, the majority of the new African states adopted a centralized system of government in an attempt to hold their new nations together, to unify their diverse ethnolinguistic, cultural, and religious societies, and to control divisions and conflicts arising from these diversities.

Rothchild (1966), in a remarkable example of the propensities of African leaders to do away with federalism as early as the 1960s, quotes a speech by Dr. Kwame Nkrumah, the president of Ghana. Dr. Nkrumah said that "in order to improve effectively and quickly the serious damage done to Africa as a result of imperialism and colonialism, the emergent African states need strong, unitary states capable of exercising a central authority for mobilization of the national effort and the coordination of reconstruction and progress. For this reason, I consider that even the idea of regional federations in Africa is fraught with many dangers. There is the danger of the development of regional loyalties, fighting against each other[89]."

While the advent of federalism in Africa could be traced back to the colonial era, Nigeria and Cameroon emerged into independence with federalism as their preferred form of state. In 1972, however, Cameroon conducted a constitutional review that resulted in the replacement of federalism with a unitary government. Six years after "The Year of Africa," Rothchild (1966) observed that in Africa, fed-

---

88 De Waal, 2000
89 Nkrumah, 1960

eralism has often proved to be brittle, disintegrating under pressures that surpass its reconciliatory capabilities. This has frequently led to a shift towards more centralized forms of government, either within the existing state framework or among the constituent parts of the federal state.

The resurgence of decentralization in Africa began in earnest in the 1980s. Within a decade, many countries on the continent had adopted federalism or introduced some form of power sharing at the local levels[90]. Although most of the literature in this area is patchy and case-based, there is evidence of federal governance or decentralization in countries such as Comoros, Nigeria, South Africa, Kenya, Ethiopia, Sudan, and Somalia, among others. Again, scholars have noted the tendency of new federal countries to revert back to centralization, often due to "recentralization of major infrastructure programs and shortcuts back to nationwide (unitary) politics that come through the political, administrative and financial might of the central government"[91].

The question posed by Rothchild (1966) about what accounts for the fragility of federalism under African circumstances" is still important and valid. Is it "the lack of appeal" as he put it at the time, or more to do with what Fukuyama (2004:56) describes as the institutional and political nature of "the missing dimension of stateness—that is state building"?

Research interest in contemporary federalism in Africa has rapidly increased in recent years. A number of researchers have observed the lack of comparative studies on the complexities of the continent's federal systems of governance. The case-based approach has drawn the locus of attention to the origins and forms of federalism in Africa separately for each federal nation. To a lesser extent, research has looked into the political, legal, and institutional struc-

---

90 Erk, 2014
91 Erk, 2014

tures of federalism in Africa and its impact on the continent's diverse communities, cultures, and ethnicities.

3.4. FEDERALISM AS A RESPONSE TO POST-CONFLICT CHALLENGES

Ethiopia's implementation of federalism represents an innovative response to its complex ethnic landscape. Transitioning from centralized, authoritarian regimes, the nation embraced a federal system in 1995, granting substantial autonomy to ethnically defined regions. This approach, termed "ethnic federalism," sought to provide self-governance for Ethiopia's diverse ethnic groups within their respective regional states. The Ethiopian federal model has achieved notable successes, enabling the preservation and expression of diverse cultural and linguistic identities. Granting ethnic groups control over their affairs has mitigated ethnic tensions in some areas and bolstered minority participation in national politics[92].

However, the Ethiopian model has also encountered critical challenges. It has unintentionally solidified ethnic divisions, making ethnicity a more prominent factor in political and societal spheres. This situation has occasionally sparked inter-ethnic conflicts, especially in mixed-population regions. Additionally, the power dynamics between the federal government and regional states have frequently been a source of tension, with central government overreach concerns and doubts about regional governance capacities[93].

In contrast, post-apartheid South Africa's approach to federalism, marked by its 1996 constitution, emphasizes cooperative federalism. This framework aims to harmonize national unity with acknowledgment of cultural and regional diversity. South Africa's federalism has been key in maintaining unity post-apartheid and in preventing the centralization of power. The provinces have autonomy in certain domains like education and health, which facilitates regionally

---

92 Vaughn, 2003
93 Aalen, 2006

tailored policies. This approach has also diffused political tensions, allowing diverse political parties to wield power at provincial levels. Yet, South Africa's federal system also confronts challenges. Ambiguities in national and provincial government responsibilities have led to inefficiencies and conflicts. Furthermore, stark economic disparities between provinces, such as those between wealthier Gauteng and the Western Cape and less affluent regions, exacerbate regional inequalities[94].

Ethiopia and South Africa demonstrate the potential of federalism to manage ethnic and regional divides. Ethiopia's federalism has provided ethnic groups a platform for self-expression and governance, which is crucial for a nation with a history of ethnic marginalization. In South Africa, federalism has facilitated the accommodation of linguistic and cultural diversity within a unified national framework, aiding the transition from an apartheid state to a democratic one. Federalism's efficacy in these scenarios lies in its capacity to recognize and integrate diversity, enabling governance structures where various groups' identities are reflected and heard. This aspect is particularly potent in post-conflict societies where tensions often arise from lack of recognition and representation.

Despite challenges, federalism in both Ethiopia and South Africa has contributed to relative political stability and ethnic coexistence. In Ethiopia, federalism has provided ethnic groups a pathway to self-determination within a united framework. In South Africa, it has supported the peaceful coexistence of a culturally diverse populace. However, the limitations are significant. In Ethiopia, the politicization of ethnic identities has at times aggravated conflicts rather than resolving them. In South Africa, while federalism has achieved political accommodation, it still grapples with economic disparities and social inequalities[95].

---

94 Steytler, 2017
95 Manor, 1999

3.5. INSTITUTIONAL DESIGN AND IMPLEMENTATION OF FEDERAL SYSTEMS

Federalism in Africa displays a rich tapestry of forms, each customized to the distinctive historical and sociopolitical landscapes of the individual countries. The constitutional framework is pivotal, providing the foundational principles and structures for state governance. In African nations, constitutions are often crafted to accommodate and reconcile the diversity of ethnic, linguistic, and cultural groups, and to establish systems for sharing power and allocating resources. For example, Ethiopia's 1995 constitution, which heralds its ethnic federal system, notably recognizes ethnic groups' rights to self-determination, including the option of secession. In contrast, Nigeria's constitution emphasizes decentralizing power to states, allowing them autonomy in managing their affairs while sustaining a robust central government. These frameworks underscore federalism's legal underpinnings, clearly demarcating the powers and responsibilities at various government levels[96].

Central to these constitutional frameworks is the intricate balance between national unity and regional autonomy. Legal stipulations must adeptly tackle governance issues, jurisdictional matters, and fiscal federalism, all while respecting the autonomy of the federative units. This entails establishing legislative bodies at different tiers, defining the scope of their legislative competencies, and outlining mechanisms for revenue sharing and conflict resolution.

International entities and organizations frequently play a pivotal role in nurturing and fortifying federal structures, particularly in post-conflict scenarios. Support from these actors can take many forms, such as offering expertise in constitution drafting, building the capacity of government officials and civil society, and providing financial aid for infrastructure development.

Organizations like the United Nations, the African Union, and various regional alliances have actively engaged in peacekeeping and

---
[96] Suberu, 2001

nation-building in post-conflict African nations. In South Sudan, for instance, international actors have been integral to the ongoing peace negotiations, which encompass deliberations on embracing a federal system to accommodate the nation's ethnic diversity. These international actors also act as mediators in disputes between regional and central governments, creating forums for dialogue and negotiation. Additionally, global financial institutions such as the World Bank and the International Monetary Fund often link funding to governance reforms, including decentralization and the adoption of federal structures[97].

However, challenges abound in implementing federal systems in post-conflict African countries. A primary concern is deficits in institutional capacity, as post-conflict nations often struggle with weakness in the state structures essential for managing complex federal systems. Challenges include inadequate human resources, insufficient infrastructure, and poor service delivery. Other hurdles are the persistent legacy of mistrust and ethnic divisions. While federal systems seek to manage these divisions by granting autonomy to ethnic or regional groups, such autonomy can sometimes exacerbate divisions and even fuel secessionist movements, as seen in some regions of Ethiopia[98].

Decentralization, a key aspect of federalism, can also present challenges. Determining the right degree of autonomy, powers, and resources for regional governments requires careful calibration. Excessive decentralization might weaken central authority and lead to fragmentation, while insufficient decentralization can perpetuate marginalization among certain groups[99]. Economic disparities also impact the stability of federal systems. Equitable distribution of resources and economic opportunities is crucial for the stability of federal systems. In countries with resources unevenly distributed

---

97 Collier, 2003
98 Asnake, 2013
99 Watts, 2008

across regions, this can lead to conflict and competition among federative units[100].

3.6. IMPACT OF FEDERALISM ON POLITICAL STABILITY AND GOVERNANCE

Federalism can profoundly shape democratization processes by fostering more inclusive and participatory governance models. In federal systems, power is distributed rather than centralized, often resulting in governance that is closer and more responsive to people. This decentralized power structure can bolster political involvement at local levels, empowering citizens to impact policies directly affecting their communities.

Moreover, federal frameworks offer minority groups a crucial voice in national political discourse; this is especially significant in ethnically diverse nations. By providing representation across multiple government tiers, federalism can enhance the legitimacy of the political system and mitigate feelings of disenfranchisement among minority groups.

In terms of promoting democracy, federal structures act as safeguards against power centralization, reducing the risk of authoritarian regimes. The division of powers between different levels of government establishes checks and balances that are crucial for preventing power abuse and upholding democratic tenets.

A critical element of federal systems is the power equilibrium between central and regional authorities. This balance is essential for federation stability and functionality. Overcentralization can negate federalism's benefits, while excessive regional autonomy might cause state fragmentation and weaken national cohesion.

Successful federal systems strike a balance in which both central and regional governments wield adequate power to execute their roles. Typically, central governments manage national concerns like

---

100 Kimenyi, 2017

defense and foreign policy, while regional governments address local issues such as education and healthcare. This division of responsibility should be clearly outlined in the constitution to avoid conflicts and overlaps in authority[101].

In Africa, several countries have adopted federal systems and have experienced varying challenges and levels of success:

Ethiopia. Ethiopia's ethnic federalism has been pivotal in managing ethnic diversity, granting these groups regional governance and thereby fostering autonomy and reducing ethnic conflicts. However, this system has also been criticized for deepening ethnic divisions and sparking tensions, particularly in ethnically diverse regions[102].

Nigeria. Nigeria's federal structure has played a crucial role in managing its vast ethnic and religious diversity. Allowing regions to exercise autonomy has been vital in a country with more than 250 ethnic groups. Nonetheless, resource distribution, especially oil revenue, remains a contentious issue, causing regional disparities and conflicts[103].

South Africa. Post-apartheid South Africa has utilized federalism to promote unity while acknowledging cultural and regional diversity. The federal system has facilitated power decentralization and ensured governance participation from all racial and ethnic groups, significantly contributing to political stability and fostering national unity[104].

Federalism, as demonstrated in these contexts, provides a framework to acknowledge and manage diversity, playing a vital role in the democratization process. By empowering local governance, ensuring minority representation, and maintaining a check on power

---

101 Anderson, 2008
102 Asnake, 2013
103 Suberu, 2001
104 Steytler, 2005

concentration, it contributes to stable, inclusive, and participatory political systems.

3.7. FEDERALISM AND SOCIOECONOMIC DEVELOPMENT

Federalism significantly influences socioeconomic development, particularly in regions emerging from conflict or marked by diversity. It decentralizes governance, enabling the formulation of economic strategies that are more responsive to localized needs and priorities. This decentralized model is particularly effective in revitalizing regions where centralization has previously resulted in neglect or poor resource management and aligns development initiatives with specific local requirements[105].

A key advantage of federalism is its promotion of decentralized economic policy-making. By actively involving local governments and communities in economic decision-making processes, federalism ensures that development strategies are finely tuned to the unique conditions of each region. This localized approach fosters the formulation of economic activities that cater to the specific strengths and needs of different regions[106].

In Nigeria, for instance, the federal system has facilitated a more equitable distribution of revenues from oil production. The implementation of the derivation principle, where oil-producing states receive a significant share of the revenue generated from their resources, exemplifies an economic policy aligned with regional resource availability. This approach has been crucial in addressing economic disparities among regions and in promoting localized investment and growth[107].

Ethiopia's experience underscores how federalism can foster economic competition among regions, encouraging them to leverage

---

105 Daniel, 2007
106 Smoke, 2003
107 Suberu, 2001

their unique attributes, as with the agricultural potential in Oromia and the manufacturing capabilities in Amhara. Such internal competition has been instrumental in driving economic development at both the regional and national levels[108].

However, challenges exist in the application of federalism, particularly within fiscal management in African contexts. South Africa's experience illustrates the difficulties in managing disparities arising from uneven distribution of natural resources across regions. The implementation of efficient revenue-sharing mechanisms and equalization grants is vital in ensuring equitable development across all regions[109].

Moreover, federalism impacts the provision of social services and infrastructure. By enabling regional governments to tailor services such as education and healthcare to their specific needs, as seen in Tanzania, federalism can lead to enhanced outcomes in these vital sectors. It also allows regions to prioritize infrastructure development based on local needs and economic priorities, contributing to more balanced regional growth and mitigating urban-rural divides[110].

In the realm of poverty reduction, federalism empowers local governments to launch targeted initiatives that address region-specific causes of poverty. This localized approach to economic development, supported by region-specific policies, can lead to more effective strategies for reducing poverty[111].

The role of federalism in socioeconomic development across various countries demonstrates its capacity to harmonize regional diversity with overarching national economic goals. While federalism provides a structure for regional autonomy and resource distribution, it must also tackle challenges like ensuring equitable development and maintaining regional independence. The effectiveness

---

108 Asnake, 2013
109 Steytler and Mettler, 2001
110 Manor, 1999
111 Collier, 2003

of federalism in fostering socioeconomic growth is contingent on its adaptability to the distinct economic, political, and social environments of each nation. Ongoing adaptation and responsive governance are essential in optimizing the benefits of federalism to ensure that it serves both national unity and regional prosperity effectively.

3.8. ETHNO-POLITICAL CONSIDERATIONS IN FEDERAL STRUCTURES

Federalism offers a pragmatic approach to managing ethnic diversity, particularly in areas where ethno-political tensions are prominent. By granting ethnic groups autonomy within their designated regions, federal systems can cultivate empowerment and representation. This autonomy is crucial for preserving distinct cultural and linguistic identities, which might feel endangered under a highly centralized regime[112].

The principle of self-governance inherent in federal systems can mitigate tensions by ensuring that decisions impacting local communities are made by those deeply acquainted with and integral to these communities. Moreover, federalism can enhance the sense of belonging among various ethnic groups as they observe their rights and identities safeguarded constitutionally and their perspectives included in national dialogues. However, the effectiveness of federalism in handling ethnic diversity hinges on the system's design and execution. It necessitates a delicate balance between providing autonomy and upholding a cohesive national policy, particularly regarding national security, foreign relations, and economic progression[113].

Ethiopia's adoption of ethnic federalism in the 1990s is an illustrative example. The nation's constitution acknowledges the self-determination rights of ethnic groups, leading to the establishment of ethnically based regional states. This arrangement has empowered

---

112 Asnake, 2013
113 Fessha, 2011

ethnic groups like the Oromos, the Somalis, the Tigrayans, and the Amharas with increased self-governance. Yet it has also brought challenges, such as inter-ethnic conflicts and disputes over borders and resources[114].

Nigeria's federal model, crafted to manage its ethnic and religious diversity, is another case in point. The federal structure in Nigeria, home to more than 250 ethnic groups, seeks to distribute power equitably and prevent any group's dominance. While this system has facilitated ethnic representation, it has also encountered pressures from conflicts stemming from resource distribution, especially in the oil-abundant Niger Delta region[115].

Belgium's federal system, though outside Africa, provides an intriguing instance of managing ethnic strife. The nation's shift to federalism in the 1990s was a response to frictions between its major linguistic groups, the Flemish and the Walloons. Belgian federalism has granted these communities authority over cultural, educational, and linguistic matters, markedly easing tensions[116].

In federal structures, the acknowledgment of cultural and linguistic rights is crucial, particularly in ethnically diverse nations. These rights are vital for preserving minority languages and cultures that enrich the national cultural heritage. Federal systems often recognize cultural and linguistic rights by giving regional languages official status and permitting their use in education, the judiciary, and public administration. This acknowledgment not only sustains linguistic diversity but also ensures citizen engagement with governmental institutions in their native languages.

Additionally, federal systems can bolster cultural rights by enabling regional governments to formulate policies supporting local cultures and traditions. This might include backing for cultural festivals, traditional customs, and institutions that enrich the com-

---

114 Young, 1996
115 Suberu, 2001
116 Deschouwer, 2009

munity's cultural life. Nevertheless, safeguarding cultural and linguistic rights must be balanced against promoting national unity. Successful federal systems discover ways to celebrate diversity while nurturing a shared identity and purpose[117].

3.9. EXAMINING FEDERALISM IN ETHIOPIA, NIGERIA, AND SOUTH AFRICA

The few comparative studies of the three major federal nations in Africa—Nigeria, South Africa, and Ethiopia—reveal some similarities in the structures and objectives of their federalism. In particular, the political thought commonly referred to as "holding together" federalism has the overarching aim of combining unity and diversity, which focuses on preserving unity and territorial integrity. At the same time, this approach accommodates each country's ethnic, cultural, and religious diversity with the provision of some degree of self-governance at the local level[118].

Ethiopia's federal system, characterized by its unique approach to ethnic federalism, is primarily organized along ethnic lines. This structure, established in the 1995 Constitution, created nine ethnically based regional states and two chartered cities. The arrangement, which grants each region the right to establish its government and to adopt its official language, reflects the country's diverse ethnic composition. It aims to address the historical marginalization of certain ethnic groups, offering them political autonomy to manage affairs in such areas as education, taxation, and law enforcement. This approach marks a radical departure from centralized systems; it targets the diffusion of long-standing ethnic tensions that had been exacerbated by centralized imperial and military rule, which often suppressed ethnic diversity[119].

---

117 Fenna and Thomas, 2015
118 Watts, 2008
119 Aalen, 2006

One of the notable successes of Ethiopia's federal system is its facilitation of governance and self-administration for various ethnic groups. In contrast with past centralization and assimilation policies, this federal system has empowered ethnic groups to preserve their languages, cultures, and identities. For example, regions like Somalia and Amhara have developed their own legislative, executive, and judicial structures, aligning governance with their cultural and societal norms. Additionally, the federal arrangement has fostered stability and development in previously marginalized regions. The use of local languages in schools and the promotion of local cultures have enhanced a sense of belonging and recognition among various ethnicities[120].

However, Ethiopia's ethnic federalism has faced significant challenges. Aligning federal units along ethnic lines has heightened ethnic consciousness, sometimes overshadowing national identity. This has led to increased inter-ethnic competition and conflict, as observed in regions like Tigray, Oromia, and Somali where conflict has escalated to violence and humanitarian crises. Balancing regional autonomy with cohesive national policy, particularly in economic planning and foreign policy, remains a critical issue, as demonstrated in the Tigray conflict. The Ethiopian model, which favors geographically concentrated ethnicities, also struggles to accommodate dispersed ethnic groups; this poses a challenge in managing ethnic diversity while promoting national unity and stability.

Nigeria's federal system functions through a complex three-tiered structure consisting of the federal government, thirty-six state governments, and 774 local government areas, as outlined in the Constitution of the Federal Republic of Nigeria (1999). This constitution specifies the powers and responsibilities of each governmental level, creating a balance of authority across the federation. The federal government exercises significant powers in the critical areas of defense, foreign policy, and currency management. In contrast, state government responsibilities include agriculture, education, and health.

---

120 Vaughn, 2003

Local governments focus on community-level responsibilities such as basic education and the provision of healthcare[121].

A notable aspect of Nigeria's federalism is its fiscal arrangement, especially regarding the distribution of oil revenue, which remains a contentious issue. The derivation principle, part of this fiscal arrangement, stipulates that a portion of revenue from natural resources is returned to the originating state. This principle aims to address regional disparities but has not fully resolved tensions related to resource allocation.

Despite challenges, Nigeria's federal system has contributed significantly to maintaining national unity amid vast ethnic and religious diversity. The establishment of states and local governments has provided some local autonomy and representation, which has enhanced governance accessibility and responsiveness to localized needs. For instance, state and local governments have been pivotal in managing primary healthcare, basic education, and infrastructure development. The federal structure also allows ethnic and religious groups to participate in political processes, reducing the risks of centralized oppression. Moreover, the derivation principle in revenue sharing is an important measure to balance national interests with regional demands, particularly for oil-producing states[122].

However, Nigeria's federal system faces challenges, especially in managing the complex dynamics of resource control, ethnic and religious diversity, and the distribution of political power. Centralization of oil revenues is a major source of conflict, particularly between oil-producing states in the Niger Delta and the federal government. These states argue for a larger share of oil revenue, citing environmental damage and economic underdevelopment as justification for greater fiscal autonomy. This contention has sometimes led to militant activities, impacting national oil production and the country's broader economy. Additionally, ethnic and religious

---

121 Suberu, 2001
122 Elazar, 1987

conflicts, particularly in the Middle Belt and northern regions, pose significant challenges. These conflicts, rooted in historical grievances, are intensified by competition for political power and resources. Nigeria's ongoing challenge is to achieve a fair distribution of resources and to ensure adequate representation and autonomy for its diverse groups, while also preserving national unity[123].

South Africa's federal system, established post-apartheid in 1996, is characterized by a unitary state divided into nine provinces. Each province possesses its own legislature and executive and is led by a premier who has authority over domains that include education, health, and housing. Despite this decentralization, the national government retains considerable power, especially in fiscal matters and overarching policy. This structure aims to decentralize power, ensure national cohesion, and prevent the domination of any one region or group. The balance between national and provincial governments is crucial in South Africa's federalism and is designed to promote equitable development nationwide.

In South Africa's democratic transition, federalism has been pivotal in addressing historical injustices of apartheid. Provinces and devolution of powers were key in enhancing political inclusivity and regional representation. Provincial legislatures and governments provide platforms for local issues and for diverse community representation. The constitutional safeguards underpinning South Africa's federal system protect minority rights and ensure the fair distribution of resources. Additionally, the system allows regions to tailor policies and governance models to their contexts, fostering innovation and localized solutions[124].

Post-apartheid South Africa's federal system also faces challenges. Economic disparities between provinces, such as the wealthier Gauteng and Western Cape areas versus the poorer areas of Eastern Cape and Limpopo, lead to uneven development and service delivery,

---

123 Adebanwi and Obadare, 2013
124 Henrard, 2000

exacerbating socioeconomic inequalities. In some provinces, governance issues, including inefficiencies and corruption, undermine federal effectiveness. Moreover, balancing provincial autonomy with national unity remains complex, with tensions arising over the national government's dominant role in fiscal and policy matters. South Africa's federal challenge lies in fostering equitable development and balancing decentralization with national integration while continuing to address apartheid-era inequalities[125].

In comparison, these three cases of federalism in Africa demonstrate that while federal structures can be effective in managing diversity, they are not without their challenges. Issues such as ethnic and regional conflicts in Ethiopia, resource-control disputes in Nigeria, and economic and governance inequalities in South Africa are critical considerations. These experiences suggest that successful federalism requires a careful balancing act that is responsive to the unique sociopolitical dynamics of each country.

In conclusion, the federalism experiences of Ethiopia, Nigeria, and South Africa provide valuable insights for other nations grappling with similar challenges. They illustrate that while there is no one-size-fits-all model, federalism does offer a flexible framework that can be adapted to diverse contexts. Understanding the successes and challenges of these countries can inform and guide other nations in designing federal systems that promote unity, accommodate diversity, and foster sustainable development. This comparative analysis not only contributes to the academic understanding of federalism but also offers practical lessons for policymakers and leaders in similarly diverse and complex societies.

3.10. CHALLENGES AND CRITICISMS OF FEDERALISM IN AFRICA

The challenge of secessionism is a significant concern for federal systems in Africa. The autonomy granted to regions or states can

---

125 Steytler, 2017

inadvertently fuel separatist movements, especially in areas with distinct ethnic, cultural, or economic identities. The risk of secessionism escalates when populations perceive their ambitions to be unachievable within the existing federal framework.

In Ethiopia, for instance, the constitutional right to secession has sparked tensions and calls for independence in the Somali region[126]. Similarly, Nigeria's Niger Delta region, rich in resources, has experienced secessionist movements, propelled by feelings of marginalization and exploitation[127].

Beyond secessionism, federal systems in Africa often face regional disparities. Economic and developmental imbalances between regions can engender dissatisfaction and friction. Regions that feel neglected or unfairly treated in national resource allocation may demand more autonomy or even secession.

The balance between centralization and decentralization, which is pivotal in African federal systems, forms a core debate. This debate centers on the optimal degree of power and autonomy that regional governments should have compared to that of the central government.

Advocates for decentralization argue that it enables more responsive and region-specific governance. Yet critics warn that excessive decentralization might undermine national unity and foster fragmentation, especially in countries with pronounced ethnic or regional identities.

Conversely, proponents of centralization view it as a means to maintain cohesive national policies and mitigate regional inequalities. However, excessive centralization can foster feelings of alienation and neglect in remote or minority regions, potentially igniting secessionist tendencies.

---

126 Asnake, 2013
127 Courson, 2009

Some critics posit that federalism, often perceived as a Western political construct, may not be entirely fitting for African contexts. This argument stems from the belief that African societies have unique historical, cultural, and political experiences distinct from that of Western counterparts[128]. These critics argue that the imposition of federal structures, sometimes influenced by Western entities or international organizations, overlooks traditional African forms of governance, which are rooted in community consensus and indigenous leadership. They suggest that these indigenous governance systems might be more appropriate for African contexts[129].

Moreover, the ethnic and cultural diversity in many African countries, compounded by the legacy of arbitrarily drawn colonial borders, presents specific challenges that may not be fully addressed by Western federalism models. Critics advocate for a more tailored approach, integrating African values, traditions, and experiences into the governance framework[130].

3.11. LESSONS LEARNED AND FUTURE PROSPECTS

The efficacy of federalism in post-conflict African nations can be assessed through various criteria including political stability, ethnic and regional cohesion, economic growth, and social integration. In Ethiopia and Nigeria, federalism has been pivotal in accommodating diverse ethnic groups by granting them a degree of autonomy within a united state framework. Despite challenges, Ethiopia's ethnic federalism has enabled various ethnicities to assert their identities and to govern themselves[131]. Nigeria's federal structure has been instrumental in distributing power among its numerous ethnic groups, though issues related to resource allocation and regional disparities persist[132].

---

128 Ekeh, 1975
129 Gazibo, 2013
130 Crawford, 1994
131 Asnake, 2013
132 Suberu, 2001

Nevertheless, federalism's success is not uniformly evident. Its occasional failure to suppress secessionist movements or to alleviate ethnic strife indicates a need for more adaptable and inclusive federal solutions. Moreover, balancing regional autonomy with national coherence continues to be a challenge in many African federal states.

Adapting federal models to African realities necessitates several key conditions. Firstly, African federal systems should embrace the continent's vast cultural and ethnic diversity. African systems should potentially extend beyond typical Western federal models to incorporate governance forms reflecting African sociopolitical contexts, like integrating traditional leadership into the federal governance structure.

Secondly, it is vital to consider each African country's historical context, especially its colonial legacy. Acknowledging arbitrarily established borders that often ignored ethnic and cultural divisions is crucial, as these divisions can heighten regional and ethnic tensions within federal frameworks.

Thirdly, economic considerations are paramount. Effective federalism in Africa must tackle regional economic imbalances, guaranteeing fair distribution of resources and opportunities; this might involve innovative fiscal federalism and resource-sharing methods that consider African states' distinct economic environments.

Looking ahead, federalism's future in other post-conflict African nations hinges on several factors. A critical aspect is the readiness of political leaders and citizens to adopt federalism as a feasible governance model and to recognize decentralization's value in meeting the specific requirements of diverse groups.

International support also plays a crucial role in successfully implementing federal structures. Technical aid, facilitated dialogues, and backing for constitutional changes from international bodies and allies can significantly influence the establishment of federal systems.

Additionally, insights from current African federal states offer valuable guidance for other post-conflict nations contemplating federalism. These experiences underscore the importance of flexibility, inclusiveness, and a customized approach that addresses each country's distinct challenges and potentials

PART 2

FEDERALISM IN SOMALIA: CHALLENGES, PROGRESS AND PROSPECTS

Federalism in Somalia represents a crucial element in the nation's quest for political stability and social development following years of conflict. The adoption of federalism, enshrined in the Provisional Constitution of Somalia, was a response to the complex sociopolitical landscape of the country, marked by clan divisions, regional disparities, and the need for effective governance. This part explores various aspects of federalism in Somalia, including its historical and constitutional foundation, factors shaping its implementation, guiding tools and instruments, public awareness and impact on development, and the system's weaknesses and necessary reforms. The discussion concludes with a proposed framework for enhancing federalism in Somalia.

CHAPTER 4

FOUNDATIONS AND CONTEXTS: HISTORICAL AND CONSTITUTIONAL PERSPECTIVES

4.1. INTRODUCTION

Federalism in Somalia represents a complex and dynamic issue, one deeply interwoven with the country's turbulent history and distinctive path of constitutional development. This chapter provides an in-depth exploration of the conceptual, historical, and constitutional contexts of federalism in Somalia, shedding light on how these factors have shaped federalism's current form. It delves into Somalia's colonial past, the challenges faced in the post-independence era, and the profound effects of the prolonged civil war, all of which have significantly influenced the nation's journey toward federalism.

The focus then shifts to more recent developments, particularly the establishment of a federal system as defined in the Provisional Constitution of 2012. This includes an analysis of the constitutional underpinnings of Somali federalism and discusses how historical experiences and sociopolitical dynamics have culminated in the adoption of this governance model. The analysis, which also considers how this federal system addresses the unique challenges Somalia faces, provides a comprehensive understanding of federalism's role and significance in the nation's ongoing quest for stability and governance.

4.2. GOVERNANCE IN SOMALIA: A HISTORICAL OVERVIEW

Somalia peace and state building has been bereft of significant public awareness and debates of the historical, political, social, cultural and religious contexts in which federalism was adopted in the country as well as the reflections and decision-making processes that led to this profound shift from unitary system of government to federal political governance. This is mainly due to the pluralist and belligerent character of Somalia state building process, and the inherent tensions in emerging identity politics which compartmentalize intellectual debates into partisan political views on the congruity of federalism, or lack thereof, with our social, religious and cultural circumstances.

This section aims to outline some key historical periods and reference points in Somalia governance system to help appreciate Somalia complex and changing political landscape as a prelude to the switch to federalism. This is by no means an elaborate historical account of Somalia governance system nor is it an attempt to describe these events as harbinger to Somalia federalism.

4.2.1. From Ancient Times to Colonial Struggles

The history of the Somali people stretches back to prehistoric times, a narrative supported by archaeological findings across the Horn of Africa and corroborated by ancient Egyptian inscriptions that reference the Somali coast[133]. Known to the ancient Egyptians as "the Land of Punt," Somalia enjoyed a flourishing trade relationship with Egypt, particularly during the reign of Queen Hatshepsut[134]. The subsequent Arab and Persian settlements along the Somali coastline facilitated the spread of Islam, leading to the emergence of influential city-states such as Zayla, Berbera, Mogadishu, Merca, and Baraawe. These cities thrived as commercial hubs due to their strategic locations[135]. In 1331, the renowned Muslim traveler Ibn Battuta described Mogadishu as "a town endless in its size," noting that high-quality textiles produced there were exported to Egypt and other international markets[136].

---

133 Laitin and Samatar, 1987
134 Fitzgibbon, 1982, p. 6
135 Laitin and Samatar, 1987
136 Battuta, 1975: 13–15

In pre-colonial Somalia, despite the absence of a permanent centralized authority, the society was organized into independent local administrations, including various sultanates and kingdoms. These entities engaged in extensive trade with the outside world, conducting commerce with Arab administrations, Egyptians, Turks, Omanis, and Zanzibarians long before the arrival of European powers[137]. These interactions involved shipments of goods and services through Somali ports, managed by sultans and territorial clan leaders acting as independent entities[138].

Several significant Sultanates and Kingdoms emerged in different parts of the Somali peninsula, each with its own geographical coverage and period of influence[139]. Notable among these were:

- **Adal Sultanate (14th-16th centuries):** Covered northwestern Somalia, Harar, and parts of Abyssinia, with its capital at Zeila.

- **Ajuran Sultanate (13th-17th centuries):** Dominated southern and southwestern Somalia, including the entire inter-river area, with its capital at Ghandershe.

- **Geledi Sultanate (17th-20th centuries):** Ruled over the lower Shabelle and upper Juba rivers until its dissolution by the Italians, with its capital at Afgoye.

- **Majerteen Sultanate (16th-20th centuries):** Controlled the eastern coast of the Somali Peninsula, known as the Horn of Africa, and its surrounding hinterlands, with capitals at Bargal and Alula.

- **Hobyo Sultanate (19th-20th centuries):** Covered central Somalia and southern parts of the Somali region of Ethiopia, with its capital at Hobyo.

---

137 Hess, 1966; Lewis, 1961
138 Hess, 1966
139 Abdi, 2024

- **Warsangeli Sultanate (13th-20th centuries):** Spanned the northeastern Somali coast and its hinterlands, with its capital at Lasqoray.

These Sultanates were centers of trade, culture, and governance, negotiating independently with external powers and contributing to the region's rich historical legacy.

European engagement in Somalia predates the late nineteenth-century colonial era, with Portuguese attacks on Somali coastal cities like Berbera, Zayla, Mogadishu, Barawe, and Merca disrupting trade and plundering wealth as early as 1518[140]. The colonization of Somalia and division of Somalia territories into five distinct territories during the nineteenth century continues to have profound impact on security and state building in the Horn of Africa. The French occupied Djibouti, formerly known as French Somaliland from 1862 to 1977, while the British controlled the northern parts, the area known as British Somaliland from 1888 to 1960 as well as a large area in the deep south populated by ethnic Somalis, known as Northern Frontier District (NFD) that was later incorporated into Kenya. The Italians, meanwhile, colonized the bulk of Somalia, including the capital, Mogadishu, from 1923 until 1960. Additionally, the Ethiopians took control of the Western Somali territory known as Ogaden and later the land of British known as "Haud and Reserved Area"[141].

Efforts to unify Somali territories frequently met with external interference, resulting in continued division under various foreign administrations. For instance, despite British Foreign Secretary Ernest Bevin's advocacy for a unified Somali administration, Britain transferred control of the Haud and Reserved Area, traditionally part of British Somaliland, to Ethiopia in 1954 without consulting the local Somali population. This move was perceived as contradic-

---

140 Cassanelli, 1982
141 Brown, 1956; Hoehne and Luling, 2010

tory to the expressed policy and spurred greater nationalist sentiment among Somalis[142].

Similarly, despite a 1962 referendum in the Northern Frontier District (NFD) showing strong local support for joining Somalia, Britain disregarded the results and incorporated the NFD into Kenya, further frustrating Somali nationalist aspirations[143]. Additionally, while southern Somaliland was placed under Italian administration as a UN trust territory, the UN imposed safeguards to protect the inhabitants, including constitutional guarantees for their rights[144].

Nationalist efforts were also fueled by historical resistance movements, accidental reunifications under Italian and later British control which were corollary of the Italian and British struggle in the Horn of Africa during the second world war, and the successful defeat of colonial powers in other regions. These factors inspired the formation of the Somali Youth League (SYL), which, along with other nationalist groups, intensified campaigns for independence despite opposition and repressive measures by colonial and Ethiopian authorities[145]. Ultimately, the persistent efforts of Somali nationalists led to the independence of several Somali territories after long struggles, both political and military.

The United Nations Charter emphasizes the self-determination of peoples, a principle echoed in the human rights covenants asserting that all peoples have the right to determine their political, economic, social, and cultural development. This principle played a crucial role in the events of 1960 when Italian Somaliland and British Somaliland merged to become the independent Somali Republic, which also recognized the right to self-determination in its 1960 constitution. However, the doctrine of *utipossidetis juris* complicated matters by requiring new states to maintain preexisting colonial borders, which often conflicted with the ethnic and cultural realities

---

142 Lewis, 1980; Samatar, 1997
143 Cassanelli, 1982
144 UNGA, 1949
145 Laitin and Samatar, 1987

on the ground. This was particularly problematic for Somalia, where arbitrary borders divided ethnic Somalis between Somalia, Ethiopia, and Kenya, sparking significant territorial disputes[146].

4.2.2. Democratic Experimentation in Somalia

In 1956, under the Italian Trusteeship agreement, the first democratic elections were held in the trust territory, former Italian Somaliland, with the Somali Youth League (SYL) securing forty-three of sixty seats. This election paved the way for Abdullahi Isse of the SYL to head the first internal Somali government, and Aden Abdulle Osman was elected as the president of the Legislative Assembly[147]. Similarly, democratic elections took place in the British Protectorate in February 1960, with the Somali National League (SNL) capturing a significant majority[148]. Post-independence, Somalia adopted parliamentary democracy, maintaining a commendable record of free and fair elections from 1960 until 1968, including several peaceful transitions of power[149].

The 1960 Somali constitution, active until the 1969 military coup, protected numerous human rights aligned with the Universal Declaration of Human Rights, including the rights to life, liberty, security, and political participation. It supported multiparty elections, voting rights, and political association[150]. During civilian rule, the judiciary remained independent, and political violence was notably absent, although corruption, nepotism, and mismanagement eventually tainted the government's reputation. The escalating tension among political elites eroded national solidarity and institutional integrity, setting the stage for military intervention due to growing public demand for change[151].

---

146 Lewis, 1980; Cassanelli, 1982
147 Lewis, 1980
148 Samatar and Samatar, 2008
149 Samatar and Samatar, 2008
150 Cotran, 1963
151 Laitin, 1976

4.2.3. The Military and Its Aftermath

Just seven months into his presidency, on October 15, 1969, President Abdurashid Ali Sharmarke of Somalia was assassinated by one of his bodyguards during a visit to the northern part of the country. This event foreshadowed significant political changes. A mere week after the assassination, on October 21, 1969, Somalia's democratically elected civilian government was overthrown in a military coup d'état, led by Major General Mohamed Siyad Barre and the Supreme Revolutionary Council (SRC). This coup abruptly ended Somalia's emerging multiparty democracy[152].

The military takeover initially garnered widespread popular support, as General Siyad Barre capitalized on a wave of populist euphoria. Many hoped the disciplined army would curb the pervasive corruption and nepotism that plagued the civilian administration and weakened state institutions. Early in its tenure, the military government focused on domestic governance improvements and extended its authority across the nation, including remote interior regions. One of its first significant acts was to adopt the Latin script for the previously unwritten Somali language, launching an extensive literacy campaign that reached both urban centers and isolated rural areas[153].

The initial enthusiasm for the military regime in Somalia quickly waned as it faced the same daunting political, social, and economic challenges that had plagued the previous government. The regime found itself recycling the same limited policy options as its predecessor[154]. It suspended the constitution and curtailed numerous civil liberties, including freedom of association and the right to habeas corpus. In 1975, the regime harshly silenced dissent by executing ten religious leaders who opposed a proposed gender equality law on the grounds that it contradicted Islamic law[155].

---

152 Payton, 1980
153 Samatar, 1988
154 Clapham, 1985
155 Laitin, 1976

Prior to the 1977–1978 border war with Ethiopia, the military government undertook several development projects without facing armed opposition. However, the situation deteriorated after Somali forces, lacking support from their communist allies, were defeated and retreated from the Ogaden region[156]. The aftermath of a failed coup attempt in 1978 by military officers led President Siyad Barre to adopt a policy of severe nepotism to maintain power at any cost[157]. The regime brutally suppressed the rebellion, executing the coup leaders immediately after a military trial, targeting their families and clan members, and intensifying the regime's repressive measures[158].

According to Cassanelli (1982), the repressive policies of President Siyad Barre marked a significant transition from populism to a more militaristic and divisive approach. John Drysdale (2001) notes that Barre learned to rely exclusively on his relatives to maintain control, leading to policies that fostered a divide-and-rule strategy. This shift contributed significantly to the all-out civil war that ensued following the regime's collapse in 1991. As the military regime increasingly resorted to coercion and oppression to retain power, there were few, if any, ideological or interest-based organizations capable of effectively challenging its authority.

The manipulation of clan affiliations was not unique to the military government; all armed factions opposing the regime also recruited members based on clan lines, further politicizing and militarizing clan politics[159]. In 1978, Majeerteen military officers established the first armed opposition group, the Somali Salvation Democratic Front (SSDF). Similarly, in early 1981, members of the Isaq clan in northwestern Somalia (now Somaliland) formed the Somali National Movement (SNM) in London[160]. By 1989, the Hawiye clan members had created another significant group, the United Somali

---

156 Laitin, 1979
157 Drysdale, 2001
158 Amnesty International, 1992
159 Adam, 1992
160 Drysdale, 2001

Congress (USC), in Rome. The emergence of these armed groups increasingly weakened Barre's hold on power, setting the stage for the country's prolonged conflict.

Ali et all (2019) narrates that uprisings and military conflicts started between 1988 and 1991 among various armed insurgents including the Somali Salvation Democratic Front (SSDF) in the northeast, the Somali National Movement (SNM) in the northwest, the United Somali Congress (USC) in the southcentral, and the Somali Patriotic Movement (SPM) in the south. On January 26, 1991, Siyad Barre was overthrown by the insurgents. The fall of Siyad Barre was followed by political struggle and civil war that saw the formation of other factions such as the Somalia National Front (SNF), the Somali Democratic Movement (SDM) and the Rahanweyn Resistance Army (RRA); this continued until 2000 when efforts to establish a federal government system took root.

During the political struggle, the breakdown of peace and order led to takeovers by war lords and later to Islamic Union Courts (IUC) due to the absence of any other conflict-resolution mechanisms within the community. When IUCs were removed from control, they morphed into al-Shabaab, who despite being defeated as a force, have formed terrorist cells and continue to create insecurity through random attacks across the country and in neighboring countries.

4.2.4. The "4.5" Power-Sharing System

Introduced at the 2000 Arta Conference in Djibouti and continuing to this day, the "4.5" system in Somalia is a political power-sharing arrangement designed to ensure representation and balance among the country's major clans. Established to promote inclusivity and prevent any single clan from dominating the political landscape after years of civil conflict, the system allocates parliamentary seats and other key government positions. The "4" refers to the four major clans—Darod, Hawiye, Dir, and Digil/Mirifle—each of whom receives an equal share of seats. The ".5" refers to a coalition of smaller clans and minority groups collectively that receive half the number of seats allocated to each major clan.

4.2.5. Somalia Governance and Political Culture Political Culture

Despite the rich historical accounts of commercial, cultural, and religious interactions between the Somali people and the outside world, the documentation of ancient governance structures and the political culture of the Somali people is markedly sparse. City-states, kingdoms, sultanates, and tribal fiefdom governance systems existed in various parts of Somali territories prior to the imperial partition of Somali society. However, the formal organization of Somali society and territories into political units and the formation of the Somali republic can be traced back to colonial rule from the 1880s[161].

Lewis characterized post-colonial African nations such as Somalia as "accidental aggregates of peoples and tribes thrown together within a single political framework by the colonial process itself"[162]. This aggregation inadvertently led to the arbitrary partition of homogenous people and tribes into different colonial governance and political systems.

Abdullahi (2020) provides a comprehensive examination of the internal dynamics and historical development of political elites in Somalia. His analysis delves into the complexities of Somali political history, offering insights into key periods, events, and socio-political configurations such as the legacy of colonial rule, post-independence challenges, military rule, and the civil war. These factors collectively contributed to the creation of a powerful elite political culture based on clan identity, significantly influencing the nation's trajectory.

The legacy of colonial rule is further explored in the context of the post-independence Somali republic grappling with the consequences of partition, particularly the struggle to forge a single political system

---

161 Laitin & Samatar, 1987; Lewis, 2008
162 Lewis, 2004: 489

from the disparate administrative systems and political cultures inherited from the British and Italian colonial rulers[163]. Despite variations in administrative structures, education, and socio-economic circumstances between the two territories, democratic governance prevailed from 1960 to 1969, although power was unevenly distributed, with political elites from Italian Somaliland beginning to dominate the political, legislative, and judicial spheres. Within these political elites, there were differing opinions on the form of government for an independent Somali state. Notably, one political party, Hizbi Democratic Mustaqbal Somali, which represented the Digil and Mirifle tribes, advocated for a federal constitution and full regional autonomy[164].

The 1969 revolutionary military coup introduced a new socio-political philosophy based on military oligarchy and termed "scientific socialism"[165]. This dictatorial regime imposed a top-down political culture, concentrating power and resources in the center. Abdullahi (2020) describes how the military regime attempted to dismantle clan politics but ultimately reinforced clan identities through strategic military and political appointments, exacerbating clan-based divisions.

The civil war and the disintegration of the Somali state into clan-based regions and territories, including the secession of Somaliland and the emergence of autonomous states such as Puntland, are other significant events that have shaped contemporary Somali political governance. In attempts to reconcile various factions and restore the Somali state, different governance models were explored, including the current experimentation with federalism. However, entrenched elite political networks with diverse political inclinations continued to dominate these processes, manipulating clannism as a political tool and reinforcing the segmentary Somali tribal identity through

---

163 Kapil, 1966
164 Eno, in ed. Osman and Souaré, 2007
165 Davidson, 1975; Laitin, 1976

the 4.5 representation and power-sharing scheme (Menkhaus, 2018; Abdullahi, 2020).

Given the varied actors and political stances, defining the political culture in Somalia is challenging, yet it remains as pluralized as the tribal divisions that have plagued the country. It is widely acknowledged that the primary challenge facing the country is finding common ground among the different political opinions—centralism, federalism, decentralization, and secessionism—which influence strategic decision-making, power and resource sharing, and diplomatic interactions.

4.2.6. Summary

Somalia's tumultuous history has been shaped by various governance systems: post-independence parliamentarianism, Siyad Barre's authoritarian regime, clan-based governance post-1991, and the modern federal approach. Each has faced formidable challenges. The reasons for their failures are complex and multifaceted, involving historical, cultural, and political factors that have interacted in ways that perpetually undermine governance efforts.

Despite varied experiments in governance, the root causes of Somalia's governmental challenges remain deeply embedded in the fabric of its society. The failure to establish a stable, inclusive political system is a testament to the complexity of reconciling historical grievances and clan identities with the demands of modern statehood. The manipulation of these clan identities, whether under colonial rule, during Barre's regime, or in the ensuing clan-based power struggles, has continuously undermined national unity and development.

Assessing whether the governance crisis in Somalia is due to the systems of governance or to the culture of the political elite is complex. The problems appear to be twofold. On one hand, each governance system has failed to adequately account for and integrate the deeply entrenched clan divisions and the sociopolitical context of Somalia. On the other hand, leadership across these systems has often been characterized by corruption, poor management, and a lack of vision, which exacerbate systemic flaws.

The introduction of a federal system in 2004 marked yet another effort to address Somalia's ongoing challenges through the decentralization of power. Nonetheless, this system too faces unique challenges and limitations. At the core of these governance failures lies the problematic culture of the Somali political elite, marked by widespread corruption and nepotism. This pervasive issue continues to thwart effective governance and hinders the development of a robust administration. Such an elite culture not only deepens systemic weaknesses but also significantly impedes sincere efforts to build a functional and inclusive governance system.

For Somalia to progress toward a stable and democratic governance structure, it must undertake comprehensive systemic reforms that not only change the political system but also the culture of its leadership and must genuinely reconcile clan allegiances and historical grievances. This approach promises a more unified national identity and a sustainable governance framework capable of fostering peace and development in Somalia.

4.3. HISTORICAL PATH OF FEDERALISM IN SOMALIA

Historically, especially between the eleventh and the sixteenth centuries, Somalis fought regional wars (Putnam and Noor, 1993). In 1869 the Suez Canal opened, paving the way for Europeans to extend their occupation farther into the region (Putnam and Noor, 1993) and Europeans began ruling the Somalis. Northern Somalia and northeastern Kenya were under the British and southern Somalia was under the Italians. The northwest—which is now Djibouti— was under the French and the Ogaden region was handed over to Ethiopia by the British[166].

Mohamed (2014) reports that the Somali people living in different Somali territories—having been divided to this extent by

---

166 Lewis, 1988

European colonialism, the emergence of the liberation movement, and the growth of Pan-Somalism—sought independence from the colonial powers. In 1948 the Independent Constitution Party was formed. This party advocated for federalism in Somalia, believing it to be the best option for a democratically united Somalia without tribal discrimination[167]. However, the plan for federalism was seen as a tool for dividing the country and was rejected.

Similarly, the elites, such as those from Digil/Mirifle clans, who proved to be among the earliest proponents of federalism in Somalia, attempted to gain independence from the Europeans in the 1950s. However, there was intense apprehension by some belonging to the Digil/Mirifle communities; they feared domination by non-Digil/Mirifle clans (those who spoke Maxaa Tiri) who would impose laws and policies on other clans the moment the Europeans left Somalia[168].

According to Anderson and Keil (2018), the colonial legacy in the Horn of Africa led to the introduction of arbitrary boundaries dividing Kenya, Ethiopia, and Somalia. These boundaries arbitrarily divided ethnic Somali people.

Ali et all (2019) describes the independence of the Somali colonies as a process where northern and southern Somalia received their independence from the United Kingdom and Italy on June 26, 1960, and July 1, 1960, respectively. The two regions then merged to form the Somali Republic on July 1, 1960, under the leadership of the first president, Aden Abdullahi Osman Daar.

The second president, Abdirashid Ali Shamarke, came to power on June 10, 1967, but was later assassinated by a member of the Somali Police Force on October 15, 1969. The assassination was closely followed by a military coup led by Mohamed Siyad Barre who promoted his "scientific socialism" as the major political and governance ideology for the development of Somalia. He aimed to fundamentally restructure the country from a clan-based traditional state

---

167 Mukhtar, 1989
168 Elmi and Barise, 2006

to a modern economy. He started radical programs to end tribalism or clannism so that people would look to the state to solve all their problems.

Ali et all (2019) explains that between 1988 and 1991 uprisings and military conflicts started among various armed insurgents; these included the Somali Salvation Democratic Front in the northeast, the Somali National Movement in the northwest, the United Somali Congress in the southcentral region, and the Somali Patriotic Movement in the south. On January 26, 1991, Siyad Barre was overthrown by the insurgents. His fall was followed by political struggle and civil war that saw the formation of other factions such as the Somalia National Front, the Somali Democratic Movement (SDM), and the Rahaweyn Resistance Army. These factions continued until 2000 when efforts to establish a federal government system took root.

During the political struggle, peace and order broke down, leading to takeovers by war lords and later by Islamic Union courts (IUCs) in the absence of any other conflict-resolution mechanisms within the community. After the IUCs lost control, they morphed into al-Shabaab and, despite being defeated as a force, formed terrorist cells and continue to create insecurity through random attacks across the south and central parts of Somali and neighboring countries.

By the year 2000, after a decade of intense civil strife, the concept of a Somali federal government began to gain traction. The idea of establishing a federal system was a recurring theme in all reconciliation efforts from 1991 to 2004. Despite numerous unsuccessful attempts to form a national government, in 2004 Somali political leaders eventually converged on the decision to establish a Transitional Federal Government. This marked the formal adoption of a federal system of governance and initiated the process of establishing federal states.

The Somali Provisional Federal Constitution, adopted in August 2012, delineates a federal government structure comprising two tiers: federal and state governments. This constitution lays the groundwork for a more inclusive and representative governance framework, aiming to ensure equal social, political, and economic representation of all groups, including minorities and marginalized communities.

The pursuit of federalism in Somalia has yielded notable accomplishments, especially in the context of establishing and reinforcing regional states. Puntland serves as a trailblazing instance in this regard. Its establishment of an autonomous administration in 1998, well ahead of the formal introduction of the federal system in 2012, positioned Puntland as a forerunner in decentralized governance. This early adoption has been influential and has provided a framework for subsequent regional states like Jubaland, Southwest, Galmudug, and Hirshabelle. These regions have played a pivotal role in fortifying the federal structure, enabling governance that is more attuned to local necessities and challenges, aspects often overlooked by centralized governance systems. The decentralization facilitated by these regional states has been instrumental in providing essential services at the local level by responding more effectively to the unique requirements of their communities.

In terms of democratic advancement, Puntland has taken significant strides, particularly with the implementation of the "one person, one vote" policy in local council elections. This move marks a considerable progression from the historically dominant clan-based, indirect voting system in Somali politics and has signaled a shift toward more inclusive and participatory governance. This initiative has not only enhanced political participation within Puntland but also set an encouraging precedent for democratization within Somalia's federal framework. The adoption of such electoral processes across other regional states is critical in cultivating a sense of civic responsibility and ownership among citizens, which in turn contributes to the stability and credibility of governance structures at both the local and the federal level.

4.4. CHALLENGES AND DELAYS IN IMPLEMENTING FEDERALISM IN SOMALIA

The implementation of federalism in Somalia has encountered substantial challenges, marked by setbacks stemming from a mix of political, social, and historical factors. These complexities have hindered the nation's transition from centralized authority to a more distributed federal system. Key among these challenges is the delay in reviewing and ratifying the Somali constitution, as noted by Abubakar (2016). Without a ratified constitution, the development of essential federal structures and processes crucial for balanced power-sharing and effective governance is stymied. Additionally, the legal and political frameworks meant to guide federalism are plagued with ambiguities and inconsistencies, leading to varied interpretations and potential conflicts, as Chevreau (2019) pointed out.

Further complicating the implementation are Somalia's unique security issues, complex constitutional and political dynamics, and the limitations of the existing federal framework. These challenges include internal conflicts, extremist threats, inter-clan rivalries, and shifting alliances, all within a fluid constitutional and political landscape that is not fully adapted to Somalia's sociopolitical and cultural realities. These factors contribute to insufficient guidance for the federalism process, a lack of comprehensive reconciliation across diverse Somali communities, challenges posed by ineffective regional administrators, and the influence of external entities, all of which exacerbate the difficulties of establishing a federal government.

The key issues impacting Somalia's federalism efforts include:

- **Historical Context and the Impact of Civil War:** The collapse of centralized governance in 1991 led to a devastating civil war and a power vacuum filled by various militia groups, warlords, and Islamist factions like Al-Shabaab. It was not until a somewhat stable government was established in 2012 that serious discussions on federalism could begin.

- **Clan Dynamics and Federalism:** Clan loyalties significantly influence Somalia's social and political landscape, often leading to rivalries that complicate federal negotiations and necessitate careful power-sharing and cooperation among competing groups.

- **Legal and Constitutional Dilemmas:** The absence of a clear and universally accepted legal framework, combined with conflicting interpretations of the provisional constitution, frequently leads to disputes and undermines governance, stalling the progress of federalism.

- **Leadership and Political Will:** Effective leadership is essential for a successful federal transition. However, Somalia has experienced intermittent lack of political will or counterproductive leadership, leading to deadlocks and hindering federal advancements.

- **Security Concerns:** Security issues, particularly those posed by Al-Shabaab, exploit the slow pace of federalism and pose constant threats to national stability and unity.

- **Economic Imbalances:** Economic disparities between more developed regions and less developed areas influence federal negotiations, affecting discussions on resource allocation and power-sharing.

- **Infrastructure and Resource Constraints:** Many Somali regions suffer from inadequate infrastructure and resources necessary for effective regional governance, further complicated by coordination challenges and overshadowed by security priorities.

- **External Influences and Geopolitical Dynamics:** International involvement in Somalia's federalism, while necessary, sometimes introduces conditions misaligned with local needs. Additionally, influences from neighboring countries and regional powers complicate the federalization process.

Understanding and addressing these diverse factors is essential for a comprehensive assessment of the progress and hurdles in Somalia's federalization efforts.

4.5. ISLAM, SOMALI CULTURE, AND FEDERALISM: AN INTEGRATED PERSPECTIVE

Islam plays a profound role in shaping the daily life and societal structure of Somalis, functioning not just as a religion, but as a comprehensive lifestyle. Its pervasive influence extends across social norms, legal frameworks, and political systems and is deeply intertwined with the fabric of Somali society.

The Islamic legal system, or Sharia, provides a foundational structure that seamlessly integrates with the traditional Somali customary law known as "Xeer." This traditional system, administered by clan elders, operates alongside formal state-backed courts. Xeer relies on a combination of precedent, Sharia law, and oral agreements between clans to resolve disputes and determine outcomes, particularly in rural regions and in areas with limited state infrastructure. In these contexts, Xeer offers an accessible, affordable, and swift alternative to state courts, which may be less accessible to many Somalis[169].

Sharia and Xeer prioritize community consensus and uphold moral obligations. Both played a crucial role in shaping local governance structures long before the introduction of federalism in Somalia. This dual legal system underscores the deep-rooted cultural and religious practices that continue to govern community life and conflict resolution in Somalia today.

The Somali Provisional Constitution, in Article 2, Clauses 1, 2, and 3, explicitly incorporates Islamic principles into state governance by designating Islam as the state religion and elevating Sharia to the supreme law of the land. This integration significantly influences the legislative and judicial processes within the country. It guides

---

169 Peterson and Zaki, 2023

the formulation of laws, influences judicial decisions, and shapes the overall political landscape[170]. This legal and political integration underscores the deep intertwining of religious principles with national governance, highlighting the unique way in which Islamic tenets are woven into the very fabric of Somali society.

Federalism, which involves the division of powers between central and local governments, provides a governance model that intriguingly corresponds with the principles outlined in Islamic teachings. The Islamic principles of justice, consultation, and communal welfare, as defined by the Qur'an and Hadith, present a rich and valuable framework for understanding and applying federalism in culturally complex societies like Somalia.

In the Islamic tradition, the concept of shura, or consultation, plays a pivotal role. Surah Ash-Shura (The Qur'an 42:38) emphasizes this, stating, "And those who answer the Call of their Lord and perform As-Salah and who (conduct) their affairs by mutual consultation, and who spend of what We have bestowed on them." The above verse of the Qur'an is the basis for participatory decision-making on which every person charged with the affairs of the community or the organization ought to adhere to (Mohiuddin and Islam, 2016). This verse promotes decision-making through collective consultation, mirroring the federalist principle of local autonomy and participatory governance. It suggests a governance structure where decisions are made closer to the grassroots level, enhancing the engagement and responsiveness of the administration to the needs of the community.

The Hadith further underscores the importance of ethical leadership within such a governance framework. The Prophet Muhammad (peace be upon him) articulated, "The best of your rulers are those whom you love and who love you, who invoke God's blessings upon you and you invoke His blessings upon them" (Sahih Muslim). This highlights the necessity for a mutual and respectful relationship

---

170 Ahmed, 2014

between the governed and their leaders. As a cornerstone of effective federal governance, it aims for accountability and transparency in administrative practices.

Moreover, justice and equity, which are central to Islamic jurisprudence, are also foundational to the philosophy of federalism. Surah An-Nisa, "Verily, Allah commands that you should render back the trusts to those, to whom they are due; and that when you judge between men, you judge with justice" (The Qur'an 4:58), emphasizes the importance of fairness and integrity. Federalism aligns with this by enabling localized governance that can be more finely attuned to the diverse needs and contexts of different regions and can promote justice and equity more effectively across the spectrum of governance.

Federalism was introduced to Somalia in 2004 as a strategic approach to reestablish stability and implement a structured governance system after decades of civil conflict and persistent clan-based territorial disputes. The adoption of a federal system was particularly appealing as it promised to respect and accommodate the intricate mosaic of clan structures and the prevailing Islamic traditions. By decentralizing power, the federal model allowed regional states to exercise certain degrees of autonomy, and enabled them to govern in ways that aligned closely with local customs and Islamic principles.

The federal structure in Somalia is meticulously designed to strike a delicate balance between the central government and regional authorities. It endows regional governments with the necessary flexibility to tailor policies and governance styles to align with local preferences and conditions, which is essential in a context as culturally and socially diverse as Somalia. The overarching goal of this system is to promote inclusivity and strengthen local governance, thereby boosting participation in political processes and enhancing the efficiency of public administration. This strategic approach not only addresses the complexities inherent in Somali society but also supports the seamless integration of traditional and contemporary governance mechanisms.

Given the significant impact of clan affiliations on social and political structures in Somalia, federalism serves to increase political participation by decentralizing power to local communities. This governance model is well-suited to Somali cultural norms surrounding decision-making and conflict resolution, which traditionally emphasize extensive consultation and achieving consensus. A typical example of this is seen in many Somali communities where it is customary to convene under a tree to discuss communal matters—a practice that epitomizes the federalist ideals of engagement and consensus.

This cultural inclination toward community consultation and collective decision-making aids significantly in the implementation of federal governance structures in Somalia. It cultivates a more cooperative and peaceful political environment by ensuring that local governance models are not just theoretically sound but also practically applicable and culturally appropriate. As a result, these models become more effective and sustainable, enabling the federal system to more effectively meet the unique needs and dynamics of Somali society.

However, the successful implementation of federalism in Somalia hinges on achieving a nuanced balance between respecting traditional clan governance systems and adapting to the demands of a modern federal structure. This delicate balance requires the crafting of federal arrangements that grant sufficient local autonomy while maintaining national unity. To accomplish this, a thoughtfully considered approach is necessary—one that leverages Somalia's rich cultural heritage and intricate clan dynamics to develop a governance model that is effective, sustainable, and harmonious.

Several key aspects require special consideration to achieve this balance. It is vital to maintain uniform Islamic legal principles across all regions to ensure coherent legal practices, honor Somali religious traditions, and support equitable nationwide governance. Inclusivity must also be a priority, particularly for traditionally marginalized communities, to ensure that all groups have a voice within the federal system. Additionally, the specific needs of pastoral communities, who are nomadic in their quest for pasture and water and lack permanent settlements, should be integrated into both local and national governance frameworks. Moreover, the roles of traditional elders, religious leaders, and other social institutions must be recognized and integrated into the governance process, effectively bridging the gap between age-old traditions and contemporary political structures.

Federalism in Somalia must be meticulously tailored to accommodate the unique cultural and social nuances of the region. Recognizing that there is no one-size-fits-all approach, it is essential to design a governance model that respects and reflects the distinctive characteristics and values of Somali society. This means developing a system capable of managing the complexities of clan affiliations and historical governance contexts while also integrating traditional practices and local wisdom. This tailored approach not only provides a robust framework for governance but also fosters social cohesion and community empowerment, crucial for national development and peace-building in Somalia.

By embracing principles such as decentralized governance, inclusivity, consultation, and justice, federalism offers a practical and adaptable framework that aligns with both Islamic teachings and Somali cultural traditions. This alignment ensures that governance is not only effective but adherent to the ethical and moral standards emphasized in Islam, while it is also deeply rooted in Somali cultural and societal norms. Through this integrated approach, federalism has the potential to significantly enhance national development and foster a more inclusive and equitable political environment in Somalia, paving the way for a stable and prosperous future.

4.6. FEDERALISM AND THE PROVISIONAL CONSTITUTION OF SOMALIA

A constitution is defined as a set of rules and institutions by which political and social order is organized and that provides a framework for the state to be governed[171]. According to Ghai and Galli (2006), the purposes of a constitution include laying the foundation for a political community and strengthening the organization of an existing political community. Constitutions direct the organization of state apparatus, such as the allocation, division, and exercise of power, and contain principles in which fundamental matters such as citizens' political, social, and economic rights are guaranteed[172]. Other purposes of the constitution relate to the ideas of limiting the power of state, establishing checks and balances, and providing security and a legal system for its citizens.

The concept of a constitution is intrinsically tied to the fundamental principle of sovereignty and governance, encompassing both the authority and legitimacy to rule. In his Security, Territory and Population lectures, Foucaoult described what he called governmentality or the modern art of government as "the ensemble formed by institutions, procedures, analysis, and reflections, the calculations and tactics that allow exercise of this very specific but albeit complex form of power, which has as its target population" (2007:108). A constitution encompasses the procedures, analysis, reflections, and tactics that not only provide the legal, political, and social basis to govern but that underpin the raison d'être, power, and mobilization of resources, institutions, and apparatus of the state.

Constitution-building describes a long-term process in which a political entity commits itself to the establishment or adoption of basic rules, principles, and values; these are in the form of a constitution that will regulate economic, social, political, and other aspects of life within it[173]. The need, timing, and purpose of constitution-making is partly dictated by historical, social, political, and economic conditions and by the contexts in which constitution-making processes are initiated in different countries around the world.

---

171 Miller, 1983
172 Hardin, 2013
173 Ghai and Galli, 2006

Charles Fombad argues that the centralizing tendency of post-independence African leaders, which fueled repressive governments, has given rise to the search for new approaches to ensure fundamental human rights and democratization through decentralization and the constitution-making movement in Africa. But this did not all result in constitutionalism and respect for the rule of law which "remains an ideal rather than a daily practice"[174]. This argument is especially relevant to Somalia as evidenced in the historical and political journey of Somalia's constitution-building.

4.6.1. Somalia's Constitution-Building Process

Kingdon's (1995) three-stream model provides a framework for analyzing how the drafting of Somalia's Provisional Federal Constitution was initiated and developed. The *problem stream* describes how the idea of a constitution was characterized as a high priority; it was pushed out front in the national agenda-setting to inspire action while the country was reeling with conflict and many other challenges. The *politics stream* deals with the political context, power relations, and actors, whereas the *policy stream* focuses on the process through which the constitution was developed and on the impact of the other streams on the constitution's content (the provisions and articles within the constitution).

Somalia's constitution-building was precipitated as the consequence of two decades of brutal dictatorial regime and a prolonged period of internecine conflict and statelessness. These had created, on one hand, an atmosphere of mistrust and wide divisions between the state apparatus and the Somali public who struggle to identify unifying civic values. On the other hand, they created tyrannical tendencies in the center that hindered the reconstituted post-conflict Somali state to redefine its role and win the support of the citizens.

The drafting of the Provisional Federal Constitution was initiated in 2006 when Somalia's Independent Federal Constitution Commission was established as mandated in the Transitional Federal Charter

---

174 Fombad, 2018:195

of 2004. The drafting was justified by the need for a written set of rules that could promote trust among the Somali people and restore national unity, political identity and stability, nation-building, and development. It was posited that it was necessary to normalize peace and reconciliation outcomes focused on restoration of statehood and national unity while simultaneously addressing the existing divisions within Somali society through decentralization of power.

There were three main actors in the constitution-building process: the Transitional Federal Government, representing the nation as a whole in the 4.5 representation formula; Puntland State, which was the only existing viable federal member state; and Somalia's international partners. While the traditional elders played a significant role in the formation of the Transitional Federal Government, their role in the constitution-building process, particularly in the drafting stage, was not clear. However, the constitution-building process played out at the intersection of two tendencies: central power as represented by the Transitional Federal Government and advocates of power dispersion, decentralization, and localization to the peripheries (regions and districts) as represented by Puntland State.

In August 2012, a National Constituent Assembly conference was finally convened in the Somalia capital of Mogadishu by the then–Transitional Federal Government to adopt a new Somali provisional federal constitution. This constitution contains multiple provisions about Somali federalism, the powers and roles of the different levels of the government, and mechanisms to facilitate interactions and cooperation among them.

4.6.2. Key Provisions of the Provisional Federal Constitution

Article 1 of the 2012 Provisional Federal Constitution declares that "Somalia is a federal, sovereign, and democratic republic founded on inclusive representation of the people, a multiparty system and social justice"[175]. As the first article of the constitution, its purpose

---

175 PFC, 2012:1

is to enshrine the status of Somalia as a sovereign state on the world stage and to establish its new political governance configuration in a federal system. It is the most important article in the constitution in relation to the explicit constitutional proclamation of federalism in Somalia.

Clauses in Article 4 stipulate that: (i) "After the Shari'ah, the Constitution of the Federal Republic of Somalia is the supreme law of the country. It binds the government and guides policy initiatives and decisions in all sections of government; (ii) Any law, or administrative action that is contrary to the constitution may be invalidated by the Constitutional Court, which has the authority to do so in accordance with this Constitution"[176]. These clauses enshrine the supremacy of the Provisional Federal Constitution as the law of the land and at the same time mention the Constitutional Court as the instrument that will adjudicate the compliance of the laws with the PFC. This proclamation effectively precludes any challenges to the provisions in the Constitution, safeguarding the political federal structure of the country. This entrenches federalism within the Provisional Federal Constitution, making it inviolable unless this declaration is amended.

The provisions in the PFC in relation to federalism and federal principles are outlined in several chapters of this book. Chapter 5 focuses primarily on the devolution of the powers of state powers in the Federal Republic of Somalia, which are pivotal in reorganizing the state's institutions. However, this devolution also generates significant controversies and contradictions within Somalia's federal system, as discussed in detail later.

4.6.3. Federal Structures and Levels of the Government

Article 48, Clause (1), stipulates that "In the Federal Republic of Somalia, the state is composed of two levels of government: (a) Federal Government of Somalia (FGS) level, and (b) Federal Member States (FMS) level, which is comprised of the Federal Member State

---

[176] PFC, 2012:1

government, and the local governments"[177]. This clause enshrines federalism and federal principles in the constitution for two levels of government. Article 48 is the third-most important article in the constitution in terms of enshrining federalism and federal principles; it recognizes de jure the federal principles of two levels of government in the Federal Republic of Somalia but also mentions a third level of authority (local government) that will be subsumed under the FMS. Article 48 provides the constitutional basis for Somalia's political system of government by specifying the actions of dividing the structure of state governance into levels. The acknowledgment of local governments (regions and districts) in terms of decentralization of power is significant as it is a direction to subsume them under the FMS level.

Article 50 further enshrines the principles of federalism in the Provisional Federal Constitution. It also embeds competence-based division of power, roles and responsibilities, intergovernmental relations and cooperation, consultation, and resolution of disputes through dialogue. It is the second most important article in terms of the adoption of federalism in Somalia as it provides the constitutional basis for negotiated sharing of power and resources. It balances the division of power between the two levels with standardization and equity. It implicitly reinforces the principle of intergovernmental cooperation "that of two levels of government, none subordinate one to another"[178] but describes these as working together in their sphere of competence and in the spirit of unity. However, Clause (b) of Article 50 is vague regarding federal principles; its wording, "the power is given to the level of government where it is likely to be most effectively exercised"[179], does not specify criteria or any other framework for the division of power but rather indicates an intention to defer.

---

177 PFC, 2012:13
178 PFC, 2012:14
179 PFC, 2012:14

4.6.4. Formation of the Federal Member States

Article 49, Clause 6, states that "based on a voluntary decision, two or more regions may merge to form a Federal Member State" (PFC, 2012:14). This clause stipulates that the establishment of a federal member state involves the simple criterion of two or more regions merging. It is one of the most contested clauses in the Provisional Federal Constitution. While it provides the legal basis for the establishment of an FMS, which can only consist of two or more regions, it does not specify any other criteria or the strategy, process, direction, leadership, or implementation of FMS formation.

The intention of the drafters in excluding anything less than two regions has been questioned. For instance, this clause was used by some groups to oppose the formation of Galmudug state as it did not meet the two-region criteria (Galmudug consists of one region—Galgaduud—and half of the Mudug region). This clause was also used to block the FMS aspirations of the Hiiraan region, forcing it to merge with the Middle Shabelle region to form Hirshabelle state. The clause is also a major legal hurdle to communities in the Banadir region (where the capital Mogadishu is located) in seeking FMS status. Critics have argued that it is wrong to restrict the size of a federal unit to two or more regions while proponents point out that the restrictions were intended to prevent the unsustainable proliferation of federal member states.

Clause 2 of Article 49 also describes the formation of federal member states, stating that "no single region can stand alone. Until such time as a region merges with other region(s) to form a new Federal Member State, a region shall be directly administered by the Federal Government for a maximum period of two years"[180]. While this clause has emboldened the adoption of federalism, at the same time it has given the regions free hand to form federal member states without seeking permission, input, or endorsement from the federal government.

---

180 PFC, 2012:14

4.6.5. Boundary Preservation and Social Cohesion

Furthermore, Article 49, Clause 5, calls for the preservation of the boundaries of the administrative regions as they existed before 1991 to promote social cohesion and to prevent further fragmentation and conflict. The constitutional provisions in Article 48 and Article 49 have been breached as: (i) one region and half of another region have merged and formed a FMS, and (ii) the boundaries of the pre-civil administrative regions have been changed. The aspiration and feasibility of these provisions were not debated sufficiently because they were recognized to be impractical and futile, as in the case of Puntland and Galmudug, each of which controls parts of a single region. Similar changes to the boundaries of two other pre-civil war regions (the Togdheer and Sanaag regions) were also known at the time the constitution was drafted.

4.6.6. Intergovernmental Relations and Cooperation

Article 51 directs intergovernmental relations and cooperation between the levels of government and provides the constitutional basis for decision-making as a collective responsibility through inclusive politics and cooperation between levels of government; this is a further entrenchment of federalism in Somalia. Article 51 envisions cooperative federal relations as a form of federalism and provides the legal basis for forums to advance those cooperative federal relations. This article also underlines the centrality and supremacy of the constitution in relation to other laws and State constitutions, and it gives directions to the FGS and to member states to comply with the national constitution, cautioning them against exercising powers outside of their limits. This article can be interpreted progressively to discourage claims of exorbitant powers by any level of government.

Furthermore, it instructs the formalization and institutionalization of the interactions between the two levels of the government and provides the federal parliament with the power to legislate political matters that could be subject to negotiation between the levels of government. At the same time, it minimizes the judicialization of politics by setting parameters for the negotiated settlement of disputes through written guidelines.

4.6.7. Allocation of Powers and Resources

Article 54 stipulates that "the allocation of powers and resources shall be negotiated and agreed upon by the Federal Government and the Federal Member States (pending the formation of Federal Member States), except in matters concerning: (i) Foreign affairs; (ii) National defense; (iii) Citizenship and immigration; and (iv) Monetary policy, which shall be within the powers and responsibilities of the federal government" (PFC, 2012:16). This article has caused controversies as subnational entities such as Puntland and "Somaliland" have engaged in paradiplomacy in the context of international cooperation whereas the FGS regards foreign affairs as its exclusive domain and interprets this article as a blueprint to exclude member states from international cooperation and as a tool to diminish their existing subnational paradiplomacy. The FGS also regards international trade and investment agreements as part of foreign affairs and has blocked or delegitimized trade and investment agreements between member states and foreign entities.

As a federal member state, Puntland State has had its own armed forces (Darwish, Anti-terrorism Security Force) and has resisted the integration of these forces into the national army under the jurisdiction of the FGS. The FGS, on the other hand, continues to build the Somalia National Army and receives military assistance and training from Somalia's various international partners. The different, fragmented security forces of the federal government, the FMS, and regions could destabilize the country and disturb the rebuilding, reorganization, and reform of fragile political and government institutions.

Article 53 states that: (i) "in the spirit of inter-governmental cooperation the Federal Government shall consult the Federal Member States on negotiations relating to foreign aid, trade, treaties, or other major issues related to international agreements" and (ii) "where negotiations particularly affect Federal Member State interests, the negotiating delegation of the Federal Government shall be supplemented by representatives of the Federal Member States governments"[181]. These clauses provide the legal basis under which the FMS have demanded involvement in foreign aid and international agreements. Although this passage has been interpreted differently by FGS and FMS, it is clear from the wording of the provisions that it was intended to "open up" a space of influence for member states in foreign relations and international cooperation.

The clauses of this article have caused some controversy and created a political chasm between the FGS and member states on several occasions. Their design indicates that they were intended to allay the concerns of some member states, particularly Puntland, regarding foreign aid, relations, and international cooperation and to build trust between the levels of government by promoting collaboration and transparency between them. It is worth remembering that the drafting of the Provisional Federal Constitution took place at a time of increasing subnational paradiplomacy, specifically by Puntland and "Somaliland," in the context of the globalization of Somalia's domestic issues such as piracy and the effects of global issues, such as the war on terrorism, on the domestic policies in Somalia.

A closer examination of the design, wording, and juxtaposition of Articles 53 and 54 reveal that they were intended to be positively interpreted together, especially in relation to foreign aid, trade, and international agreements. However, the two articles do not define or elucidate foreign affairs, foreign aid and trade, foreign investment and international agreement. Instead, they create contradiction and confusion whereby foreign affairs is the exclusive power of the FGS which must also ensure the participation of FMS in this sphere.

---

181 PFC, 2012:16

4.6.8. Financial Management Framework

Article 124 gives directions to the conduct of financial management. It states that "a law enacted by the Federal Parliament shall provide the framework for financial management"[182]. This article defers financial management matters to legislative action by the federal parliament. Article 50 (f) states that "the responsibility for the raising of revenue shall be given to the level of government where it is likely to be most effectively exercised"[183]. This article provides the legal basis for the shared responsibility of raising revenue, which implicitly gives a role to federal member states in financial management. The obscurity surrounding the powers of the FGS and FMS in revenue raising and financial management for their respective levels is one of the main stumbling blocks to fiscal federalism.

Financial management has become a key issue in the negotiations between the FGS and member states in four fronts: (i) resource and revenue-sharing negotiations; (ii) programs to meet the financial-management reform conditions set by the World Bank for budgetary and other financial supports; (iii) international aid where the FGS is the recipient as well as a conduit for fund transfers to FMS; and (iv) the debt relief program of the International Monetary Fund under the enhanced Heavily Indebted Poor Countries Initiative.

4.6.9. Powers of Existing Federal Member States

Article 142, Clause 1 states that "until such time that all the Federal Member States of Somalia are established, and the adopted Federal Member State Constitutions are harmonized with the Somali Federal Constitution, the Federal Member States existing prior to the provisional adoption of this Provisional Constitution by a National Constituent Assembly shall retain and exercise powers endowed by their own State Constitution"[184]. This clause recognizes the powers exercised by existing member states and legitimizes the continuation

---

182 PFC, 2012:44
183 PFC, 2012:14
184 PFC, 2012:54

of the use of such powers until all member states are formed and the constitutions are harmonized with the Provisional Federal Constitution. The mention of existing federal member states is an implicit reference to Puntland State, which was the only viable FMS prior to the adoption of the Provisional Federal Constitution.

This clause has caused a lot of controversy over the powers exercised by the federal member states, particularly by Puntland State. Puntland's constitution grants it state powers in paradiplomacy and international cooperation, such as entering trade and investment treaties, participating in international conferences, and collaborating with foreign states on issues of mutual interest. These paradiplomatic interactions have created friction between the federal government and Puntland. Puntland uses this clause as the constitutional basis for operating independently from the federal government in this sphere. Critics argue that Puntland State is part of the FGS and should not have been given preferential treatment in the constitutional design. Proponents argue that it was imperative to protect the only functioning FMS—Puntland—in the uncertain and ever-changing political and security landscape in Somalia and to thwart the extreme concentration of powers in a central government in Mogadishu that could control the legislature and the judiciary.

Article 142, Clause 2 directs that "existing Federal Member States must be consulted in the decision-making process regarding the federal system, and security arrangements"[185]. The clause ensures a space for political and security decision-making for existing member states as part of the peace and state-building initiatives in the federalization of Somalia.

4.6.10. Conclusion

There are several gaps and ambiguities in the Somalia Provisional Federal Constitution in relation to federalism and federal principles. Somalia federalism is at a critical stage at the moment. It requires a pragmatic constitution with strong emphasis on greater participation

---

185 PFC, 2012:54

by the society to reconstruct the government's political structures and to derive laws from the prevailing social and cultural norms. There is a need for certain clarity and relevance in the definition and division of powers between the two levels of the government, for institutionalization of intergovernmental relations, and for bringing people together to build trust and share ownership, thereby providing for an independent, effective, and fair justice system and law enforcement institutions.

CHAPTER 5

FACTORS SHAPING FEDERALISM IN SOMALIA

5.1. INTRODUCTION

This chapter delves into the diverse factors that shape federalism in Somalia. It draws from identified knowledge gaps, reviews of published reports, and insights from focus group discussions (FGDs) and key informant interviews (KIIs). This comprehensive approach has identified seven factors as important in shaping federalism in Somalia:

i. Federalism deals with political division and mistrust;
ii. Federalism is hampered by weak institutions and resource constraints;
iii. Federalism is promoted by peaceful regions;
iv. Federalism helps overcome national fragmentation;
v. Federalism accommodates all parties and groups;
vi. Federalism is favored by Somali people who have a strong affiliation to their region; and
vii. Federalism is favored where development in some Somali regions improved following the fall of unitary governance.

The assessment of these factors is based on data from a survey of members of the public and other sources, including desk reviews, FGDs, and KIIs. These influential factors span a range of historical, social, demographic, economic, political, and institutional considerations. Understanding these factors is crucial as they provide the foundational framework for analyzing and interpreting the findings of the rest of this study. The detailed results of this analysis, which explore the multifaceted aspects influencing federalism in Somalia, are presented in the following sections of this chapter.

5.2. OVERVIEW OF THE FACTORS SHAPING FEDERALISM

The public survey assessed people's opinions as to the relative importance of the seven factors identified as shaping federalism in Somalia. Using a standard 5-point Likert method, respondents expressed their agreement or disagreement with the identified factor. Figure 4 shows public survey responses regarding these factors.

Respondents generally agreed with the proposed factors as shaping federalism. One exception was regarding whether federalism accommodates diverse ethnic and cultural groups and differences; 51% either disagreed, were neutral or provided no feedback on this factor. There was high concurrence on two of the seven factors: federalism is hampered by weak institutions and resource constraints (74%), and federalism is favored by people who have a strong affiliation with their region (73%).

Respondents generally agreed with the identified factors, but there were different levels of convergence of opinion across the six regions. Among those from Banadir, however, there was no distinct pattern of agreement or disagreement; the only factor with which more than half of the Banadir respondents agreed was that people who were affiliated with their regions favored federalism. More respondents agreed with this factor in each of the six political regions surveyed. On the other hand, Puntland and Jubaland had a higher number of respondents who agreed with all seven factors; these were followed by Galmudug, then by Southwest and Hirshabelle.

Factors Shaping Federalism - All responses aggregated (%)

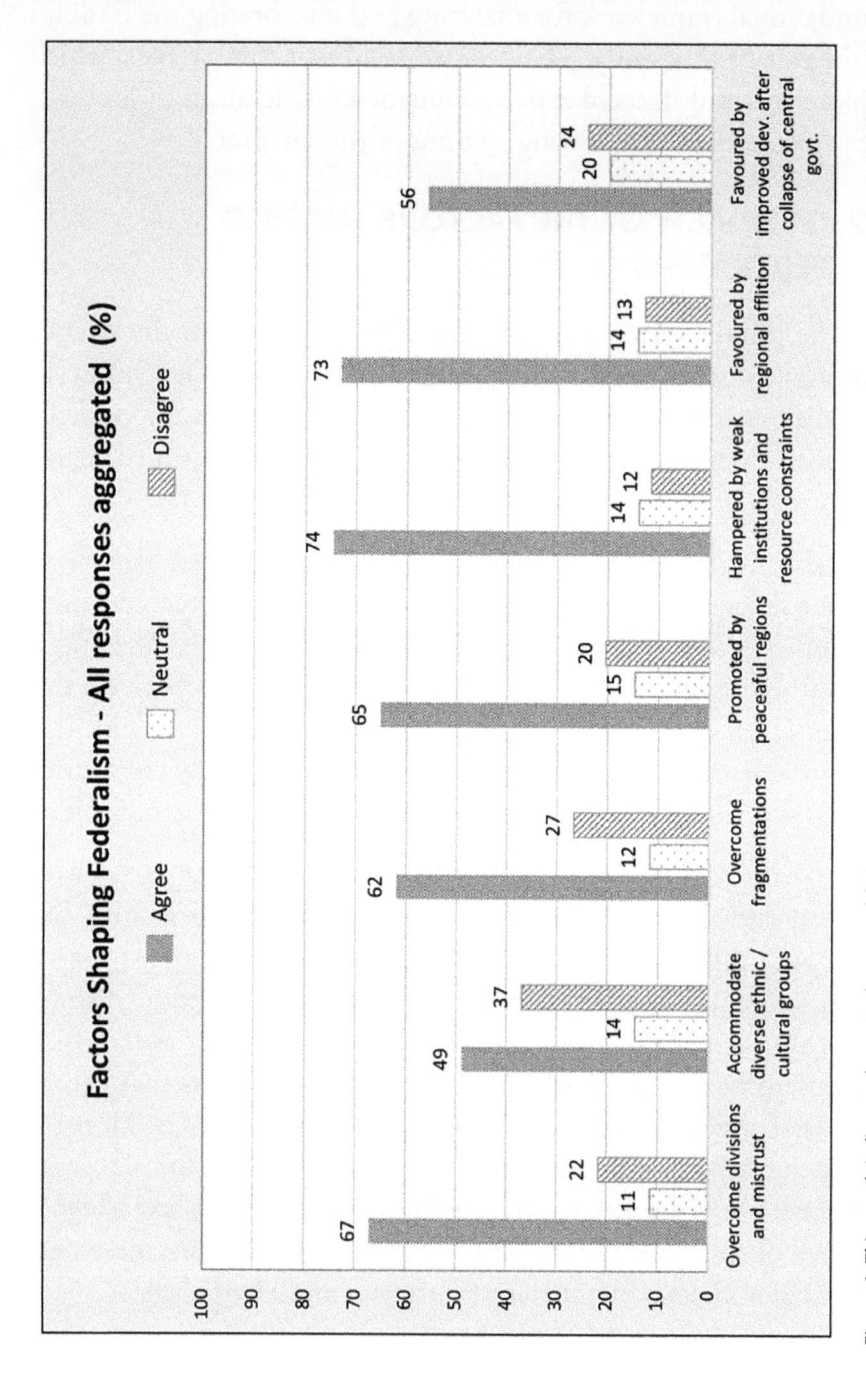

Factor	Agree	Neutral	Disagree
Overcome divisions and mistrust	67	11	22
Accommodate diverse ethnic / cultural groups	49	14	37
Overcome fragmentations	62	12	27
Promoted by peaceful regions	65	15	20
Hampered by weak institutions and resource constraints	74	12	14
Favoured by regional affilition	73	13	14
Favoured by improved dev. after collapse of central govt.	56	20	24

Figure 4. This graph indicates the attitudes toward federalism expressed by 384 respondents to a survey conducted August–October 2021 in Somalia.

The remainder of this chapter explores further the information obtained on respondents' attitudes toward factors shaping federalism in Somalia as reflected in published reports, FGDs, and KIIs.

5.3. FEDERALISM DEALS WITH POLITICAL DIVISION AND MISTRUST

The first factor identified as shaping federalism in Somalia is its potential to overcome the division and mistrust among the Somali people caused by prolonged political instability, insecurity, and civil strife. In the public survey, a majority of respondents in five of the six regions surveyed agreed with this factor. In Banadir, only 25% of respondents agreed.

With federalism enshrined in the provisional constitution, there is a high expectation that this approach will address the long-standing political division and mistrust[186]. The framework for the establishment of federal states, as provided in the provisional constitution, addresses the concerns of the Somali people regarding the possibility of a few dominant clans or groups holding executive power across Somalia[187]. To ensure structured implementation of the federalism governance system in Somalia and to deal with political division and mistrust effectively, federalism was formally proposed in the discussions of the provisional constitution. These discussions, which started at the Mbagathi Peace Process in Kenya that created the Transitional Federal Government in 2004, paved the way for the establishment of a Somalia federal government[188].

By enshrining federalism in the constitution, Somali political leaders hoped to put an end to the conflict and political unrest that had continued for more than two decades and to move toward a transparent governance system that would build strong institutions for a responsive and efficient government. Federalism studies

---

186 Ali, Dahir and Hersi, 2019
187 Chevreau, 2019
188 Klay, 2015

have observed that political instability and civil strife, which had continued for a long time, made the changes required in a post-conflict environment more difficult to implement. It would take time to transform and shift away from the established status quo, with many challenges and barriers along the way. The expected challenges and barriers, however, would influence the effectiveness of the federal system but not the governance system itself[189].

Even as the provisional constitution has enshrined a federal governance system with two levels of government as a solution to the political problems in Somalia, studies of the Somalia federalism process have highlighted important contradictions in the provisional constitution[190]. For example, in Clause 1 of Article 49, the number of federal member states are determined and their boundaries assigned as a role of the lower house of parliament while Clause 6 of the same article provides for two or more regions to voluntarily merge to form a federal member state. Such duplication of responsibility needs to be addressed to avoid conflict that may result from misinterpretation of roles.

Dahiye (2014), in assessing published information, found that the acceptance of federalism as the system to deal with political division and mistrust is strengthened by the experience of the Somali people in the unitary government systems that followed independence. In these systems, power, wealth, and services were concentrated at the center with no concern for the needs of Somalia's many diverse regions[191]. In this regard, Chevreau (2019) argues that the success of the system will depend on how it will realize the desired health relationship and balanced power sharing between the federal government and federal member states.

FGD participants observed that the federal governance system aims to deal with the entrenched political division and mistrust resulting from the past unitary government, prolonged civil strife,

---

189 Abubakar, 2016
190 Mosely, 2015
191 Dahiye, 2014

and conflict. They also highlighted the fact that real conciliation efforts to properly address the wounds and concerns of the Somali people have not been made. Further, FGD respondents raised the need for federalism to avoid the abusive actions of the Siyad Barre regime and cited the experience of the Puntland State, the autonomous entity in the northeast, where a federal type of governance has led to peace since 1998.

KIIs further confirmed the information obtained from reviews of published reports and FGDs indicating that federalism is viewed as an important approach to address political division and mistrust in Somalia. Information from the KIIs indicated that, as a result of the failures and suppressive policy of the Siyad Barre regime, Somalis could no longer trust the centralized administration; this distrust led to political instability within the government and was followed by civil war.

A federal system helps the two levels of government agree on power sharing with sufficient power devolved to the federal member states. Federalism also clearly delineates the roles and responsibilities that stay with the federal government. Furthermore, over the past few years both the federal government and the member states have instituted the National Leadership Forum (NLF) as a platform for discussion of key issues rising from federalism. This forum has created a mechanism to deal with differences and to fast-track the federalism process in Somalia. It should be noted that some representatives in the federal parliament may believe that devolving power to the regions and districts through the federal member states may reduce their political space.

5.4. WEAK INSTITUTIONS AND RESOURCE CONSTRAINTS HAMPER FEDERALISM

The second factor proposed as shaping federalism in Somalia is the history of the weak institutions and resource constraints that have hampered it. A majority of respondents in five of the six regions surveyed agreed with this factor but in Banadir only 36% agreed.

The findings of this research study strongly support the concept of weak institutions and resource constraints as a factor shaping federalism in Somalia. An analysis reveals six components of this concept: (i) weak control of the federalism process, (ii) limited capacity to implement the federalism process; (iii) weak capacity for collaboration among key institutions and stakeholders; (iv) poor definition of federalism's objectives or poor understanding of the objectives; (v) influence of the past clan-based political systems; and (vi) slow progression of the process. The dimensions of these six components are briefly elaborated upon below.

Weak institutions and limited resources have led to poor control of the federalism process in Somalia. Despite the aspiration in Somalia's provisional constitution for a federal governance system, the realization of this desire has been constrained by the limited influence and control the federal government has had in large areas of the country outside its capital, Mogadishu[192]. This lack of control has led to continuing conflict among clans over political power and resources except in regions that have managed to avoid tribal rivalry. This conflict weakens the federalism process within the federal government and between it and the federal member states and other parties. Further, due to weak institutions in Somalia, the federalism process has depended on external support to drive the process forward. Despite clear benefits witnessed from external support—for example, the creation of the peaceful implementation environment for federalism through the African Union Mission to Somalia (AMISOM)—the big questions remain: How does this external support shape the outcome of the federalism process in Somalia? How does one ensure that the interests of the parties funding and supporting the process do not override the aspirations and needs of the Somali people?

Due to weak institutions and resource constraints, implementation of the federalism process in Somalia has been chaotic. Due process has not always been followed nor have the constitutional

---

192 Klay, 2015

mandates been fully implemented[193]. In this environment, where conflicts among stakeholders can easily arise, there is an increasing shift from adhering strictly to the "doing-it-right" principle toward advancing the process to influence and achieve set targets within the federalism framework.

In a post-conflict environment such as Somalia where federalism is a continuously evolving process of "lesson learning," weak institutions and resource constraints further complicate implementation. However, these challenges also help mature the process. An example of this occurred when Jubaland, aspiring to become a full member state, was involved a tussle with Mogadishu over a claim to Gedo, Lower Juba, and Middle Juba. The outcome set an important precedent for settling constitutionality debates in practical terms, further showing the limits of the parties' political power[194].

Analysis of interviews with key informants indicates that the federalism process, which has been largely top-down, has failed the lower levels such as the districts. Hence a bottom-up approach should be adopted to ensure inclusion of all parties at all levels. Similarly, the process must be ensured at two levels: (i) a high-level process between the federal government and the member states as well as between member states, and (ii) a low-level process among districts and local communities within the member states.

A further dimension of weak institutions and resource constraints is a weaker capacity for collaboration with key institutions and stakeholders and therefore poorer coordination of the process. The political elite have different interests depending on whether they are inclined to the federal government or the member states; this creates distrust among parties who need to work collaboratively for the success of the process[195]. Further, the legacy of warlords remains, creating fear that dominant clans could use federalism to install militia to secure their leadership positions in the federal member

---
193 Klay, 2015
194 Mosely, 2015
195 Mosely, 2015

states. Equally concerning is the capacity of the federal states to effectively manage internal disputes.

Key informants have reported that federalism in Somalia should lead to a decentralized system with greater inclusion and representation of all Somali in political affairs. However, the process must not be confused with the goal of an all-inclusive political system[196]. It is clear that the federalism process is viable, although under stress, but its viability should not be mistaken for the desired goal of political inclusion and representation. The federalism process is strengthening institutional capacity and the state-building process, but questions remain regarding the effective inclusion of all parties at all levels and regarding the legitimacy of the process.

Past history and clan influences affect the capacity of institutions and the implementation of the federalism process. In member states, the process may be influenced by previous experiences and historical relationships. For example, Puntland State is formed largely by the Darod clan who share a historical relationship, but this is not always the case. In contrast, the Southwest state is inhabited by different clans who do not share a historical relationship.

Lastly, weak institutions and resource constraints have affected the progress and results of the federalism process. Starting from the Mbagathi peace conference that took place from 2002 to 2004, progress has been very slow and has taken a long time through many phases from initial peace negotiations, to the transitional government, to the federal government. The process has taken a lot of effort, time, and financial investment to initiate, to become meaningful, and to produce genuine results. This may contribute to a shift from the "doing-it-right" principle with its broader participatory processes to a focus on elite-led frameworks in the desire to see quicker progress[197].

---

196 Mosely, 2015
197 Mosely, 2015

5.5. PEACEFUL REGIONS PROMOTE FEDERALISM

The third factor identified as shaping federalism in Somalia is the strong promotion by regions such as Puntland that have experienced peace under a federalism governance arrangement. In the public survey, 78% to 100% of respondents in Puntland, Galmudug, and Jubaland agreed with this concept.

Four member states (Galmudug, Hirshabelle, Southwest, and Jubaland) have been formed successfully and there is evidence of political progress in regions such as Puntland and Somaliland that have practiced a form of federalism for a long time. These experiences contribute to the view of federalism as a suitable governance system for Somalia[198]. In 1998, at the height of civil and political strife in Somalia, Puntland was formed in the northeast region of the country. It is widely considered to be the first federal state in Somalia and it has been a staunch advocate for a federal system of governance[199]. The peace and development secured through federalism in this region have helped to shape this as a viable form of governance system for Somalia. Notably, in 2012 during the Garowe I and II conferences, Puntland played a key role in the drafting of the provisional Somalia constitution. There is, however, evidence of earlier roots of federalism in Somalia. FGD participants were informed that federalism had been initially proposed by the Digil and Mirifle people in the 1950s. Abdiqdir Soobe led the formation of the Xisbiya political party, which championed the adoption of federalism in Somalia, advocating under the slogan "federaal fathaany," meaning "we want federalism." Furthermore, by the early 2000s, even before peace-building efforts bore fruits, a few autonomous regions (Somaliland, Puntland and Galmudug) had emerged in the north in a process of decentralization[200].

Thanks to the positive outcomes in Puntland, Somaliland, and the other regions that have adopted and established federalism as

---

198 Ali, Dahir and Hersi, 2019
199 Klay, 2015
200 Dahiye, 2014

their governance system, it can be argued that this is one area of political development that has witnessed substantial progress in the last decade despite all these challenges and difficulties that the process has encountered.

5.6. FEDERALISM HELPS OVERCOME NATIONAL FRAGMENTATION

The fourth factor shaping federalism in Somalia is the argument that it helps to overcome the national fragmentation that threatened the country following prolonged political and civil strife while avoiding the centralized authoritarian rule that the Somali people fear. In three of the regions surveyed (Puntland, Galmudug, and Jubaland) a majority of respondents agreed with this idea while in the other three regions (Southwest, Hirshabelle, and Banadir), opinions were divided among those agreeing, those disagreeing, and those who were neutral or expressed no opinion.

Research by Ali, Dahir, and Hersi (2019) indicates that all peace-building and reconciliation efforts between 1991 and 2004 proposed federalism as the solution to reunite Somalia after the entrenched mistrust and division caused by the civil war. The discussion as to the best system of governance for Somalia continued for a long time within Somalia, among Somalis in the Diaspora, and with Somalia's development partners. These discussions have indicated that federalism is a popular option and the preferred alternative to bring back peace to the battered country[201]. In unifying the nation, federalism is also seen as a solution to the evils of past unitary, centralized governance system such as that led by Siyad Barre, which negatively affected many Somalis through abusive actions and suppressive policies.

There may be different options as to the type of federalism that best suits Somalia and therefore continued discussion is needed, however, there is agreement that federalism is the best option to re-

---

201 Chevreau, 2019

construct the Somali nation[202]. While it has taken a long time for Somalia to turn away from conflict and move toward state building and constitutional and political development, the progress already made is likely to lead to stability and to end political stagnation. More importantly, the process has continued to mature and to find innovative solutions to the challenges it faces. One example is the leadership forums established in early 2015 jointly by the federal government and member state leaders as a platform to discuss power sharing and responsibilities under a federal system and to resolve any conflicts that arise.

However, key informants have highlighted in interviews that the need for a governance that could address the high level of mistrust and lack of confidence in the political system was a higher reason for adopting federalism than the fact that the Somali people believe it to be the best form of governance for the country. Consequently there are pros and cons regarding federalism and parties who are for and against it.

5.7. FEDERALISM ACCOMMODATES ALL PARTIES

The fifth factor proposed as shaping federalism in Somalia is that federalism accommodates all parties, including different clans and cultural groups. Most respondents did not agree with this factor, except those in Jubaland where there was a surprisingly high (100%) level of agreement. In the public survey, aggregated responses from all six regions indicate 49% agreed, 37% disagreed, and 14% were neutral or had no option. There was slightly more agreement in Hirshabelle (55%) and Southwest (52%).

The lower level of agreement on this factor is supported by published studies that indicate that federalism in Somalia was adopted to satisfy the needs of different clans and not to respond to the ethnic diversity and recognition of differences across Somali terri-

---

202 Abubakar, 2016

torial lands and regions[203]. The reality in Somalia in the past was one where the political majority was correlated with a clan's demographic majority and where emphasis was on cultural patriotism instead of civic identity, human rights, or democratic principles[204]. Therefore, the federalism process in Somalia must find alternative frameworks that will move away from the past and emphasize national stability. In the past, clan and cultural dynamics influenced administrative systems, such as the 4.5 clan power-sharing model, which was devised to address conflicts and ensure equitable representation. Now, in this post-conflict environment, conflicting clan and group interests challenge federalism; these need to be carefully balanced and managed in a negotiated process. Clan differences divide communities that have coexisted for many years, confining them within their respective historical clans, which adversely affects the formation and development of federal member states. For example, long-term conflict between neighboring clans in North and South Galkacyo has influenced state formation process in that region.

Interview informants highlighted the fact that the regions inhabited by diverse clans have experienced a high level of conflict, with some clans feeling segregated and marginalized by other clans. This is different in regions with less clan diversity that have a historical clan relationship among their people. There is, however, agreement that federalism is viable and applicable in Somalia despite the clan differences and conflicts. What is needed are mechanisms for dispute and conflict resolution.

5.8. THE SOMALI PEOPLE'S AFFILIATION TO THEIR REGIONS FAVORS FEDERALISM

The sixth factor relates to people's inclination toward their regions of origin. This is strengthened by the experience of prolonged political and civil strife, which has led Somalis to promote decentralization of political power to the different regions of the country.

---

203 Abubakar, 2016
204 Dahiye, 2014

A majority of survey respondents across all six regions agreed with this factor. Additionally, this factor had the second highest level of agreement (73%) in aggregated responses.

Studies of federalism in Somalia indicate that tribe and political leaders, especially regional leaders, see a federal governance system as the best method to share power and wealth fairly across Somalia[205]. On the other hand, people across Somalia have demanded regional autonomy[206] and see a federal system of governance as the solution to giving their local government greater autonomy. From experience, Somali people see a vertical system of governance with a centralized unitary state as inherently undemocratic and oppressive. People demand horizontal power structures where they can retain a degree of influence at the local level.

5.9. IMPROVED DEVELOPMENT IN SOMALI REGIONS FAVORS FEDERALISM

The seventh factor influencing federalism in Somalia is the noticeable development observed in various regions following the collapse of the central government. This trend supports the argument for federalism, suggesting that decentralized governance could foster social and economic progress.

Evidence of this perspective is seen in the results of the public survey, where 56% of respondents endorsed this view. Notably, a majority in three specific regions expressed agreement: Puntland, where 91% supported this stance, Galmudug with 56%, and Jubaland, where consensus was unanimous at 100%. This widespread support underscores the potential benefits of a federal structure that accommodates regional autonomy while aiming for national development.

---

205 Ali et al., 2019
206 Klay, 2015

5.10. OTHER FACTORS OBSERVED TO SHAPE FEDERALISM IN SOMALIA

Two additional factors have been identified as significant in shaping the federalism process in Somalia. The first pertains to perceived weaknesses in the current process, particularly its lack of inclusivity and its limited effectiveness in state-building. There are concerns that the approach fails to adequately address ongoing clan conflicts, which could potentially lead to the formation of clan militias or exacerbate existing clan and group tensions, thus increasing the risk of secession[207].

The second factor highlights the necessity of customizing the federalism system to align with Somalia's unique circumstances, incorporating insights from the experiences of other countries. Analysis from key informant interviews recommends that Somalia should meticulously evaluate various federalism models to identify the most suitable framework that addresses its specific needs and challenges.

---

207 Abubakar, 2016

CHAPTER 6

TOOLS AND INSTRUMENTS GUIDING FEDERALISM IN SOMALIA

6.1. INTRODUCTION

This chapter scrutinizes the array of tools and instruments that underpin federalism in Somalia. Through comprehensive literature reviews and initial analyses, seven tools and instruments have been identified as guiding federalism in Somalia; these have been documented and structured for further analysis. These tools include:

i. The provisional constitution as the key instrument guiding federalism;

ii. The laws and regulations of the federal government and their implication for the development needs of federal member states;

iii. Intergovernmental frameworks that facilitate development and service delivery;

iv. Laws and mechanisms for fund transfers from the federal government to federal member states;

v. Harmonized monetary and fiscal policies between the federal government and federal member states;

vi. Clear roles and responsibility for the federal government and federal member states; and

vii. Alignment of the laws and regulations of federal member states with the plans and priorities of the federal government.

These tools and instruments were rigorously evaluated using data from the survey of members of the public and were supplemented by a desk review of published reports, focus group discussions (FGDs), and key informant interviews (KIIs). This chapter presents insights and findings gleaned from this comprehensive analysis and offers a detailed understanding of the mechanisms that shape and influence federalism in Somalia.

6.2. GENERAL OVERVIEW OF THE TOOLS AND INSTRUMENTS GUIDING FEDERALISM

The public survey assessed the seven tools and instruments identified as guiding federalism in Somalia. Respondents expressed their agreement or disagreement with the proposed tools and instruments using a standard 5-point Likert scale.

Figure 5 shows the aggregated responses regarding the tools and instruments that guide federalism in Somalia. There was general agreement—more than 50% among all respondents—with all the proposed tools and instruments.

The highest levels of agreement, at 65% and 63%, respectively, were with the first two tools: the provisional constitution and clear roles and responsibilities between the two levels of government. The lowest level of agreement was regarding harmonized monetary and fiscal policies between the federal government and members states (51%); the greatest number of respondents disagreed or had a neutral response (49%).

The high percentage of neutral responses (between 20% and 28%) for all the tools and instruments assessed may indicate low levels of awareness and understanding of the roles these play in supporting federalism in Somalia.

The remainder of this chapter explores information obtained on these tools and instruments, emphasizing the contributions of previously published studies, published reports, focus groups, and interviews with key informants.

Tools guiding federalism in Somalia - All responses aggregated (%)

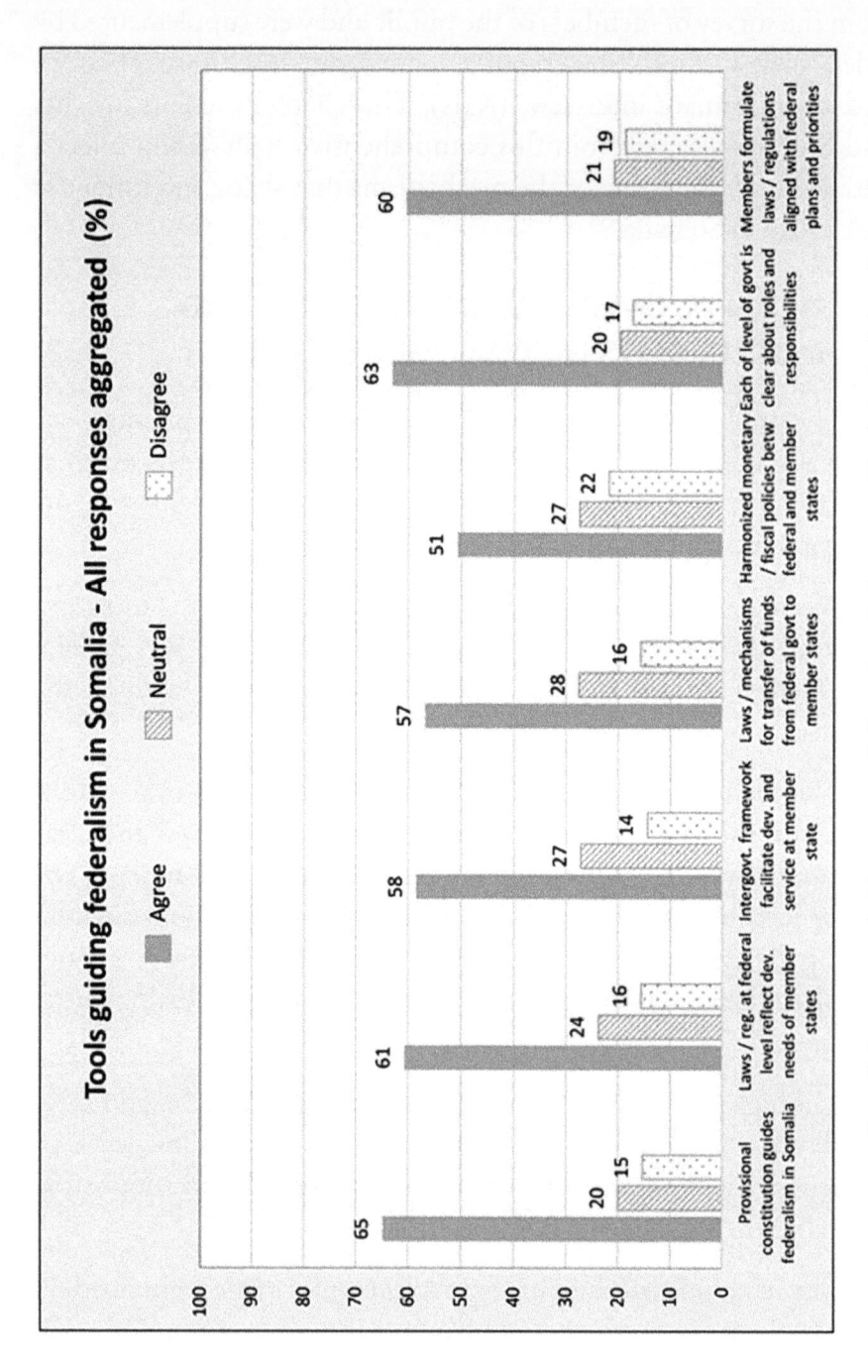

Category	Agree	Neutral	Disagree
Provisional constitution guides federalism in Somalia	65	20	15
Laws / reg. at federal level reflect dev. needs of member states	61	24	16
Intergovt. framework facilitate dev. and service at member state	58	27	14
Laws / mechanisms for transfer of funds from federal govt to member states	57	28	16
Harmonized monetary / fiscal policies betw federal and member states	51	27	22
Each of level of govt is clear about roles and responsibilities	63	20	17
Members formulate laws / regulations aligned with federal plans and priorities	60	21	19

Figure 5. Survey respondents' agreement with the tools and instruments guiding federalism in Somalia

6.3. THE PROVISIONAL CONSTITUTION

The provisional constitution has been recognized as a pivotal instrument in guiding federalism in Somalia. More than 50% of public survey respondents from three regions—Puntland, Galmudug, and Jubaland—concurred with this assessment. Conversely, in the other three regions—Southwest, Hirshabelle, and Banadir—the responses were more varied. In Southwest, a slight majority agreed with the assessment, while in Hirshabelle and Banadir, a significant portion of respondents were either neutral or did not express an opinion.

Information obtained from the KIIs and published studies on federalism support the idea of Somalia's provisional constitution as a key instrument guiding the federalism process. One key informant stated that the adoption of the provisional constitution in 2012 opened the door for the introduction of federalism as the country's preferred governance system. This key informant observed that, as a federalism instrument, the constitution has reoriented Somalia's politics from conflict between clans and political groups to a peaceful system of governance that discourages conflict. This key informant argued that the main achievement of the provisional constitution was its role in managing the strong disagreements between the political parties and building a spirit of healthy political engagement, collaboration, and partnership. As noted by Ali (2019), the constitution has created power-sharing mechanisms for federal member states and has enabled them to overcome power-sharing conflicts with the federal government.

The implementation and interpretation of the provisional constitution's federalism provisions are not easy and have faced many challenges. For example, the power-sharing model requires ongoing innovation, learning, and review. In this respect, the federal government and the member states are continuously addressing emerging challenges and learning from the federal governance systems of other countries.

KIIs informed the study that members of the constitution committee have reviewed the federalism models of many countries and have visited South Africa and Rwanda as case studies. From these visits, the committee felt that the South African system, with features that accommodate a clan-based system, is closer to what Somalia requires. In addition, the formation of the Independent Constitutional Commission within the lower and upper houses and the quarterly meetings of the commission within the federal member states strengthen the role of the provision constitution in guiding Somalia's federalism process.

6.4. FEDERAL GOVERNMENT LAWS AND REGULATIONS

The second tool that was assessed was the laws and regulations of the federal government and their implication for the federalism process and for the development needs of federal member states. Of respondents in the Galmudug, Hirshabelle, Jubaland, and Southwest regions, more than 50% agreed with the identification of federal government laws and regulations as important instruments guiding the federalism process. In Puntland and Banadir, a high number of respondents (41% and 52%, respectively) took a neutral position on this question.

Despite the agreement of respondents, this study has revealed several important dimensions relating to how the federal government's laws and regulation have affected the federalism process, its progression, and its impact on the federal member states.

Previous studies (e.g., Abubakar, 2016) have argued that federal laws and regulations have an important role in shaping federalism and have cited as examples established countries with federal systems. For instance, in the United States, individual states have autonomy and flexibility on selected areas, but the federal government remains in control of areas of national interest, such as national defense, finance, and foreign policy. Strong federal laws and regulations can establish clear directions to the member states and can promote cooperative federalism between the member states and the federal government. More importantly, as argued by one of the key informants, federal laws and regulations can help outlaw social and cultural discrimination and segregation, thereby ensuring that minority groups have equal access to government services.

Despite the importance of federal laws and regulations as a federalism tool, their application in Somalia has faced challenges. One key informant noted that there is no consistency in the application of federal laws among different member states. Another key informant observed that the judicial system faces challenges in performing its role in the federalism process because of lack of consensus on its functions between the federal government and member states, gaps within the provisional constitution, gaps within the federal laws and regulations, and differences among the various political groups.

The same sentiments were expressed in the focus group discussions where participants argued that the federal process is negatively affected by the incomplete constitution while it is also influenced by the prevailing political climate. Focus groups also observed that the federal government's laws and regulations are not yet "federalized." For example, the 4.5 formula for managing clan representation has negatively impacted the federalism process. It has created political crises and disputes between the federal government and the member states and between the president and the prime minister. These common conflicts and disagreements weaken government institutions and increase insecurity and lawlessness.

The focus group discussions recommended reforms needed to make the federalism process more effective and efficient. These include:

i. Ensuring that the federal government's laws and regulations are fully "federalized," because most existing laws and regulations do not reflect the federalism process but rather a "centralized" governance system

ii. Reviewing and completing the provisional constitution and organize a referendum for its adoption

iii. Forming a constitutional court and organize "one man–one vote" elections across the country
iv. Reviewing and finalizing the definition of the roles and responsibilities of the federal government and of the federal member states
v. Initiating a nationwide system of civic education to create awareness and explain the importance of federalism to the Somali people
vi. Developing frameworks for intergovernmental cooperation.

6.5. INTERGOVERNMENTAL COOPERATIVE FRAMEWORKS

The third tool that the study assessed was intergovernmental cooperative frameworks that facilitate the federalism process, development, and service delivery especially at the member-state level. More than 50% of the respondents in four regions (Galmudug, Southwest, Jubaland, Hirshabelle) agreed that intergovernmental frameworks were important in guiding and supporting the federalism process. In Puntland and Banadir, fewer respondents—27% and 36% respectively— agreed.

Previous studies (Mosley, 2015; Dahiye, 2014; Chevreau, 2019) identified the provisional constitution as a central and important framework guiding the federalism process in Somalia. In this process, the provisional constitutional was important for: (i) creation of the parliament and its executive structures, (ii) installation of the federalism process and its executive structures; and (iii) establishment of federal member states. However, as discussed in Section 5.3, the provisional constitution contains gaps; these areas need revision and further development, after which the constitution should be ratified. These improvements will position the constitution as a strong instrument to guide and support the federalism process in Somalia.

Another important intergovernmental framework is the National Consultative Council, a joint leadership platform established under the constitution. This framework provides a conducive environment in which the federal government and the member states can discuss and develop the policies and legal frameworks required to support the federalism process. Collaboration on peace building and state building by the federal government and the member states under the agreed federal mechanism has now led to the establishment of five federal member states.

The Mutual Accountability Framework, which brings together all state-building and peace-building actors to agree on a collective effort and plan, is another important intergovernmental framework. The plans prepared under this framework align and coordinate peace-building and state-building reforms behind a set of clear objectives.

The international community also plays an important role in supporting various intergovernmental frameworks and plans to ensure an effective federalism process. Support by the international community is provided through an agreed-upon political framework and ensures that power and resources are not concentrated in a few areas but are spread equally to strengthen governance as well as humanitarian and social services. Projects and programs supported by the international community include the Somali Dialogue Platform, the Somalia Stability Fund, and the Somali Reconciliation Framework.

Analysis of the information collected, however, indicates that gaps limit the effectiveness of the existing intergovernmental frameworks[208]. To address these gaps, it is necessary to put in place broader technical and policy frameworks. These are needed for three reasons: (i) to provide equal opportunity and support to the members states without leaving any region behind, (ii) to transform the federalism process from a delicate, imaginary idea for a majority of the Somali to something that is meaningful and tangible in their everyday lives, and (iii) to articulate and harmonize the roles and responsibilities of the

---

208 Chevreau, 2019

federal government and the federal member states. To achieve this, it will be necessary to undertake national stakeholder engagement and consultations and to organize a wide program of civic education and awareness.

6.6. LAWS AND MECHANISMS FOR FUNDS TRANSFER

The fourth tool that the study assessed was the laws and mechanisms for transferring funds and grants from the federal government to the member states. As with federal laws and regulations and intergovernmental frameworks, more than 50% of the respondents in four regions (Galmudug, Southwest, Jubaland, Hirshabelle) agreed that this was important in guiding and supporting the federalism process. In Puntland and Banadir, respondents who agreed were fewer, at 16% and 33%, respectively.

Other than the public survey, limited information was obtained on perceptions of this tool. Only one key informant stressed the need for the federal government and federal member states to work together to coordinate and distribute aid in addition to reforming the public financial and security sector and organizing the constitutional review process.

6.7. HARMONIZED MONETARY AND FISCAL POLICIES

The fifth tool assessed was the harmonization of monetary and fiscal policies between the federal government and federal member states. In three regions (Southwest, Jubaland, and Hirshabelle) more than 50% of respondents agreed that harmonized monetary and fiscal policies are important in guiding and supporting the federalism process. In the other three regions (Puntland, Galmudug, and Banadir), fewer respondents agreed: 13%, 37%, and 22% respectively.

The concept of a harmonized monetary and fiscal policy is enshrined within the provisional Somali constitution together with other important federalism pillars such as power distribution and national and regional planning[209]. However, disputes concerning fiscal management have been key issues limiting the progression of federalism.

To move the process forward, the federal government, member states, and development partners must prioritize negotiating and resolving issues related to revenue sharing and fiscal federalism. The management of resources between the federal government and the member states and among the member states has been a major challenge to the federalism process. The many dimensions to the challenge include: (i) variation in populations in the different states and regions; (ii) different levels of access to natural resources in the different regions; and (ii) financing of fiscal debt through borrowing by both the federal government and by member states[210]. The constitution and other federal laws need to address and articulate these issues clearly.

In interviews, key informants suggested several reforms to harmonize monetary and fiscal policies. These include: (i) negotiating debt relief; (ii) restoring fiscal and economic stability through the introduction of an improved financial management system; (iii) developing and adopting consistent financial regulations to mitigate contradictions that arise in the allocation of resources among the three levels of government; and (iv) improving the management and coordination of grants and aid.

These reforms will address important resource-sharing constraints and therefore move the federalism process forward. To reach sustainable results with these reforms, the federal government and member states need to work together closely.

---

209 Ali, Dahir and Hersi 2019
210 Ali, Dahir and Hersi 2019

6.8. CLEAR ROLES AND RESPONSIBILITIES FOR THE FEDERAL GOVERNMENT AND FOR MEMBER STATES

The sixth tool assessed was that of clear roles and responsibilities for the federal government and federal member states. As pointed out in Section 5.2, on aggregate, this tool had the highest level of agreement among respondents at 63% for all regions combined. In three regions (Puntland, Galmudug, and Jubaland) more than 50% of respondents agreed that clear roles and responsibilities were important in guiding and supporting the federalism process. In the other three regions (Southwest, Hirshabelle, and Banadir), fewer respondents agreed: 47%, 39%, and 17% respectively.

A previous study of the federalism process in Somalia observed that roles and responsibilities are mixed and overlapping, therefore making the implementation of federalism more complicated and prone to conflicts between political actors and stakeholders[211]. Further, one key informant noted that the absence of clear roles and responsibilities in the constitution may lead some member states or state institutions to render their services through transactions and modalities that benefit them but may be outside the constitution's framework and guidelines. Another key informant argued that the resistance by member states in implementing federalism guidelines, modules, and dialogue as required by the federal government may be attributed to a lack of genuine agreement on the roles and responsibilities of the two levels of government and a lack of mechanisms and arrangements for power sharing.

Numerous reforms have been recommended to ensure clear roles and responsibilities between the federal government and member states. These include clearly defining the powers and responsibilities of the federal government and the member states and developing a parallel but broad policy framework alongside the federalism process

---

211 Ali, Dahir and Hersi, 2019

to articulate and harmonize other subsidiary issues that relate to roles and responsibilities at all levels and among all stakeholders.

6.9. LAWS AND REGULATIONS OF MEMBER STATES

The seventh tool assessed by the study was the alignment of member state laws and regulations with the plans and priorities of the federal government. In four regions (Galmudug, Jubaland, Southwest, and Hirshabelle), more than 50% of respondents agreed that such alignment was important in guiding and supporting the federalism process. In the other two regions, Puntland and Banadir, the respondents who agreed were fewer, at 49% and 28% respectively.

In principle, as stressed by one key informant, the federalism process assumes collaboration between the member states and the federal government so that their laws and regulations are aligned and complementary. Many articles in the provisional constitution (such as Articles 50, 51, 52, and 53), provide the principles, coordination, and collaboration required to realize this alignment in laws and regulations.

Despite the need for member states to align their laws and regulations to complement the federal government, the study revealed that the process faces many challenges. First, consistency among the member states in the formulation of laws and regulation and in the application of federal laws was limited. One informant observed that some member states do not recognize federal laws and, in fact, their operations are antagonistic to the federal government. According to another key informant, there are many examples where member states have breached some articles of the constitution. Similar observations were made by previous studies that found member states had not cooperated with the federal government as stipulated in the provisional constitution[212]. In this respect, some federal member states have released press statements cutting ties with the federal government and taking up roles reserved for the federal government. Some

---

[212] Ali, Dahir and Hersi, 2019

member states captured significant levels of autonomy and power to the extent that they established complete control within their boundaries[213]. Such events have created uncertainty and threatened the federalism process as well as the unity and cohesion of Somalia.

The alignment of member states' laws, regulations, and plans is further complicated by the high costs of each member state pursuing its own governance and service delivery system and by weak, limited mechanisms for resource redistribution across the country. This has placed additional strains on a fragile system where resources are scarce[214]. A possible solution is to harmonize the federal government and member-state systems with approaches to strengthen the relationships between the two. This will reduce the costs of service delivery and bring broader peace and state-building benefits.

To address these challenges, over the past few years, the federal government and member states have established the National Leadership Forum as a platform for the discussion of emerging challenges and issues rising from the federalism process.

6.10. OTHER FACTORS THAT AFFECT THE TOOLS AND INSTRUMENTS GUIDING FEDERALISM IN SOMALIA

Additional factors affect the tools and instruments guiding federalism in Somalia. It is important to note that external support has largely determined the implementation process and arrangements as well as the establishment of different committees, forums, and intergovernmental frameworks to address emerging implementation challenges. Furthermore, local communities and clans must be involved to bring harmony and to resolve conflicts in the formation of member states and their governing bodies.

---

213 Chevreau, 2019
214 Chevreau, 2019

CHAPTER 7

PUBIC AWARENESS OF FEDERALISM AND ITS DEVELOPMENTAL IMPACT

7.1. INTRODUCTION

This chapter closely examines how federalism is perceived and understood in Somalia, in particular its ramifications for the nation's development. It assesses the public's awareness of federalism and explores the implications of this awareness for Somalia's advancement and governance structures.

Using data from the public survey, the review of published reports, and the information obtained from focus group discussions and key informant interviews, this study considers two main aspects of the public's awareness of the federalism system: (i) their preferred governance system for Somalia, and (ii) their preferred power-sharing arrangements between the federal government and member states. The data collected reflects other dimensions of the Somali peoples' awareness of federalism and its' impact on development. This chapter presents in detail the findings and insights obtained from this in-depth analysis.

7.2. AWARENESS OF THE PREFERRED GOVERNANCE SYSTEM

Figure 6 shows results of public survey responses as to their preferred governance system for Somalia. It indicates that the Somali people have a high level of awareness and preference for federalism, with more than half of the respondents (52%) identifying this system as the most suitable for Somalia as compared to a decentralized system (27%) or a unitary system (21%).

The public survey data also captured the reasons respondents prefer federalism. These reasons include political stability (63.0%), better service delivery (60.2%), economic development (60.2%), good governance (55.2%), equitable power sharing (54.7%), and prevention of dictatorships (50.0%). Other reasons cited include conflict resolution, preservation of national unity, and regional autonomy—but these had fewer responses. These results clearly indicate that the Somali people are significantly aware of federalism and its potential benefits.

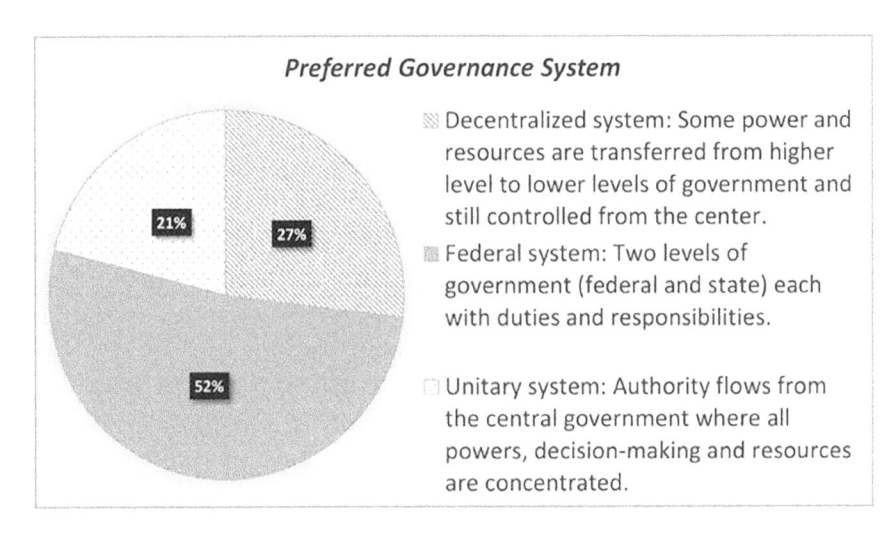

Figure 6. Public survey results indicating respondents' preferred governance system for Somalia

Chevreau (2019) observed that, although the level of awareness of federalism among Somali people was very high, there was a lack of clarity regarding the system's features and its practical operation. The population's limited understanding of these features means that some people believe the system to be an external, foreign idea aimed at dividing the people rather than uniting them; this lack of clarity could determine the long-term success or failure of federalism.

Klay (2015) also found that, despite significant support for federalism as a form of governance, the Somali people's understanding of its intricate features and functions remained extremely low, identifying a need for robust civic education and a campaign to inform and educate the people on the different aspects of federalism and its practical application. Dahiye (2014) argued that the process of drafting and discussing the Somali constitution and the federalism process had been reserved for the political elite, leaving out the common people. As a result, the Somali people had limited understating of the details of the federalism governance system. Dahiye recommended organizing civic education to raise Somali awareness of the issues pertaining to federalism and the constitution.

7.3. AWARENESS OF POWER-SHARING ARRANGEMENTS

Citizens in six regions of Somalia were surveyed as to their opinions on fifteen different areas where power might be shared between the federal government and federal member states. Their responses are summarized in Table 2.

The areas assessed to be identified through a desk review of previous federalism studies in Somalia and of the initial results of focus groups and interviews. The bold numbers in the columns in Table 2 indicate where more than half (>50%) of respondents favor particular power-sharing arrangements. Clearly depicting respondents' power-sharing preferences, this data provides a snapshot of regional consensus.

Table 2 also indicates significant variation in power-sharing preferences, both between and within regions. Those in Galmudug and Hirshabelle exhibited the highest consensus, with more than 50% of respondents agreeing on power-sharing arrangements across all fifteen areas. Those in Jubaland and Puntland, where consensus was reached in fourteen areas, followed closely. Respondents in Southwest showed agreement in ten areas, while those in Banadir agreed least, with consensus in only three areas.

Table 2. Respondents' opinions on fifteen different areas of power sharing

		\multicolumn{6}{c}{Somalia Regions}
		Puntland	Galmudug	Jubaland	Southwest	Hirshabelle	Banadir
1. Foreign Affairs	Don't know	0.0%	0.0%	0.0%	0.0%	0.0%	0.0%
	Concurrent Powers	4.7%	0.0%	0.0%	14.1%	1.6%	3.1%
	Federal Government	**95.3%**	**98.4%**	**100.0%**	**53.1%**	**81.3%**	**71.9%**
	Federal Member States	0.0%	1.6%	0.0%	32.8%	17.2%	25.0%
2. National Defense	Don't know	0.0%	0.0%	0.0%	1.6%	3.1%	4.7%
	Concurrent Powers	17.2%	11.1%	0.0%	9.4%	1.6%	10.9%
	Federal Government	**82.8%**	**87.3%**	**100.0%**	**50.0%**	**79.7%**	**67.2%**
	Federal Member States	0.0%	1.6%	0.0%	39.1%	15.6%	17.2%
3. Policing	Don't know	0.0%	0.0%	0.0%	1.6%	9.4%	6.3%
	Concurrent Powers	**56.3%**	**50.8%**	0.0%	4.7%	1.6%	18.8%
	Federal Government	37.5%	38.1%	**100.0%**	**57.8%**	**68.8%**	29.7%
	Federal Member States	6.3%	11.1%	0.0%	35.9%	20.3%	45.3%
4. Environmental Protection	Don't know	0.0%	1.6%	0.0%	3.1%	6.3%	7.8%
	Concurrent Powers	**62.5%**	**63.5%**	4.6%	4.7%	3.1%	25.0%
	Federal Government	9.4%	25.4%	**90.8%**	**56.3%**	**73.4%**	29.7%
	Federal Member States	28.1%	9.5%	4.6%	35.9%	17.2%	37.5%
5. Monetary Matters	Don't know	0.0%	1.6%	0.0%	9.4%	6.3%	6.3%
	Concurrent Powers	9.4%	6.3%	0.0%	4.7%	3.1%	17.2%
	Federal Government	**90.6%**	**92.1%**	**100.0%**	**53.1%**	**68.8%**	**45.3%**
	Federal Member States	0.0%	0.0%	0.0%	32.8%	21.9%	31.3%
6. Social Development	Don't know	0.0%	0.0%	0.0%	3.1%	1.6%	10.9%
	Concurrent Powers	48.4%	**73.0%**	12.3%	4.7%	4.7%	25.0%
	Federal Government	3.1%	12.7%	38.5%	**54.7%**	**73.4%**	25.0%
	Federal Member States	48.4%	14.3%	**49.2%**	37.5%	20.3%	**39.1%**
7. Construction of Roads and Highways	Don't know	0.0%	0.0%	0.0%	3.1%	3.1%	6.3%
	Concurrent Powers	**53.1%**	**63.5%**	1.5%	10.9%	4.7%	31.3%
	Federal Government	14.1%	31.7%	**86.2%**	**53.1%**	**76.6%**	29.7%
	Federal Member States	32.8%	4.8%	12.3%	32.8%	15.6%	32.8%
8. Construction of Ports and Airports	Don't know	0.0%	0.0%	0.0%	7.8%	6.3%	4.7%
	Concurrent Powers	**51.6%**	41.3%	0.0%	15.6%	4.7%	32.8%
	Federal Government	35.9%	**54.0%**	**100.0%**	**48.4%**	**73.4%**	25.0%
	Federal Member States	12.5%	4.8%	0.0%	28.1%	15.6%	**37.5%**
9. Immigration and Border Control	Don't know	0.0%	0.0%	0.0%	6.3%	12.5%	14.1%
	Concurrent Powers	4.7%	17.5%	0.0%	10.9%	4.7%	21.9%
	Federal Government	**95.3%**	**81.0%**	**100.0%**	**50.0%**	**67.2%**	**42.2%**
	Federal Member States	0.0%	1.6%	0.0%	32.8%	15.6%	21.9%
10. (a) Revenue Raising – Corporate Taxes	Don't know	0.0%	0.0%	0.0%	9.4%	6.3%	6.3%
	Concurrent Powers	**56.3%**	39.7%	0.0%	7.8%	6.3%	23.4%
	Federal Government	31.3%	**55.6%**	**100.0%**	**48.4%**	**67.2%**	25.0%
	Federal Member States	12.5%	4.8%	0.0%	34.4%	20.3%	**45.3%**
10. (b) Revenue Raising – Customs Taxes	Don't know	0.0%	0.0%	0.0%	4.7%	10.9%	9.4%
	Concurrent Powers	**67.2%**	30.2%	6.2%	15.6%	9.4%	26.6%
	Federal Government	12.5%	**52.4%**	**83.1%**	**46.9%**	**65.6%**	**43.8%**
	Federal Member States	20.3%	17.5%	10.8%	32.8%	14.1%	20.3%
10. (c) Revenue raising – Local Taxes	Don't know	0.0%	0.0%	0.0%	6.3%	10.9%	12.5%
	Concurrent Powers	29.7%	28.6%	12.3%	14.1%	6.3%	14.1%
	Federal Government	3.1%	9.5%	10.8%	**48.4%**	**65.6%**	17.2%
	Federal Member States	**67.2%**	**61.9%**	**76.9%**	31.3%	17.2%	**56.3%**
11. Commerce	Don't know	0.0%	0.0%	0.0%	6.3%	14.1%	7.8%
	Concurrent Powers	**53.1%**	**66.7%**	10.8%	10.9%	7.8%	29.7%
	Federal Government	39.1%	27.0%	**53.8%**	**51.6%**	**68.8%**	25.0%
	Federal Member States	7.8%	6.3%	35.4%	31.3%	9.4%	37.5%
12. Foreign Investment	Don't know	0.0%	0.0%	0.0%	9.4%	12.5%	10.9%
	Concurrent Powers	28.1%	6.3%	0.0%	17.2%	7.8%	28.1%
	Federal Government	**70.3%**	**90.5%**	**100.0%**	**48.4%**	**65.6%**	**32.8%**
	Federal Member States	1.6%	3.2%	0.0%	25.0%	14.1%	28.1%
13. Planning and Inter-national cooperation	Don't know	0.0%	0.0%	0.0%	1.6%	14.1%	7.8%
	Concurrent Powers	34.4%	12.7%	0.0%	12.5%	4.7%	26.6%
	Federal Government	**62.5%**	**87.3%**	**98.5%**	**53.1%**	**70.3%**	**35.9%**
	Federal Member States	3.1%	0.0%	1.5%	32.8%	10.9%	29.7%
	Clear preference (#)	14	15	14	10	15	3

For the four power-sharing areas, respondents clearly preferred to have the federal government control foreign affairs, national defense, monetary matters, immigration and border control, and planning with international cooperation; more than 50% of respondents indicated this preference. Local tax collection was the only area where a majority of respondents preferred that the federal member states have control; even in this category, only four of the six regions (Puntland, Galmudug, Jubaland, and Banadir) recorded more than 50% of the respondents as preferring it.

A majority of respondents preferred powers to be shared concurrently between the federal government and federal member states in the areas of policing, environmental protection, development of state-level infrastructure, and commerce.

Social development was the area with the least consensus regarding power sharing, although with more regions preferred control by federal member states. Banadir and Southwest recorded lower levels of concurrence in shared power. Responses were divided among the four power-sharing arrangements for most of the fifteen areas of power sharing, although Puntland and Galmudug showed similar patterns.

One key informant stated that the federalism process helped the federal government and the member states to agree on power-sharing arrangements, devolved powers to member states, and delineated the roles and responsibilities of the federal government. This informant further observed that the reform of the provisional constitution will allow a power-sharing arrangement that is politically agreed upon by both the federal government and the member states.

Klay's (2015) study noted that a majority of Somali people were aware of federalism and viewed it as the most suitable form of governance because it facilitates reasonable power sharing between clans, enabled regional autonomy, and contributed to reducing conflicts. Another study[215] indicated that federalism power-sharing arrange-

---

215 Abubakar, 2016

ments had been introduced in Somalia following prolonged conflict and civil war and had added value through sustainable peace and political stability, which was the initial objective for introducing the system. This study noted efforts to streamline the system and cited examples such as the leadership forum established in 2015. The forum, a joint initiative of the federal government and regional state leaders, was created as a platform to discuss issues related to power sharing and roles and responsibilities under a federal system. The young system of federal governance faced many barriers, especially as it was replacing a system of centralized governmental and clan power sharing that had existed for nearly three decades. In this regard, one key informant observed that the greatest barrier to the implementation of a full-fledged federal system of governance is the traditional clan system of governance and the complimenting 4.5 power-sharing formula under the clan reconciliation model. Furthermore, the Somali provisional constitution is under review. Until the constitution is completed and agreed upon, it will be difficult to design appropriate structures and processes that address the fundamental issues of power sharing and constructive political competition between the federal government and the member states[216].

7.4. FEDERALISM'S IMPACT ON POLITICAL DEVELOPMENT

The data collected and analyzed by this study indicate that—despite many challenges—big, positive political impacts have resulted from the adoption and initiation of a federal governance system in Somalia.

Information from key informants indicates substantial progress has been made in establishing a healthy political environment for peace and state building. Following the initiation and establishment of the federal government, four member states have been established: Jubaland, 2013; Southwest, 2014; Galmudug, 2015, and Hirshabelle, 2016. Each has established its own local institutions. The ministries

---

216 Abubakar, 2016

responsible for constitutional affairs were established at the federal level and in member states. The provisional constitution was nationally endorsed, and the Boundaries and Federation Commission was established. Other institutions formed include the National Leadership Forum (NLF), the National Consultative Council (NCC), and the Independent Constitutional Review and Implementation Commission (ICRIC); all these enable a conducive environment for the federal government and member states to prepare, negotiate, and implement policies and legal frameworks to promote a federal governance system within Somalia.

The observations of focus group participants were similar to those of the key informants, confirming the opportunities that the federal system has presented in terms of political development in Somalia. The participants highlighted the establishment of the Upper House of Parliament, which represents the interests of federal member states, as demonstrable evidence of political stability at the federal and member-state levels. This is further evidenced by the successful formation of four member states through a peaceful transfer of power. These developments indicate increasing acceptance of a federal system among the Somali people. One key informant commented that the four member states formed through the federal governance system have continued to strengthen their institutions and governance structures and to deliver services to their citizens.

The positive political development impacts revealed by key informants and focus groups participants were also evident in published studies. Chevreau (2019) noted that through the process of implementing federalism, member states have captured significant autonomy and power to the point where they have full sovereignty within their jurisdictions. Moreover, if successful, federalism has the potential to effectively create an equitable power-sharing arrangement between the federal government and member states, thereby avoiding chances that regions within Somalia regions advocate for secession. Ultimately, this may be the strongest appeal of a federal governance system for the broader Somali population.

Despite these positive political impacts, one key informant observed that the prevailing political environment has limited the performance and effectiveness of the federal governance system and of the constitutionally mandated institutions and commissions that have been established. This informant suggested changes are required to accelerate positive political development, in particular the completion of the review of the provisional constitution. This informant argued that the constitutional review process is the key strategy through which equitable power sharing was possible and other contentious issues could be fully addressed. Similarly, another key informant observed that the process of deepening federalism in Somali is directly related to the finalization of the provisional constitution and to key political agreements, including those describing the structure of the member states and the distribution of power.

Although the political impacts of the federalism process may be difficult to quantify given the challenges that surround its implementation, the information collected in this study point toward many positive impacts.

7.5. FEDERALISM'S IMPACT ON SOCIAL AND ECONOMIC DEVELOPMENT

As with political development, the data and information collected and analyzed in this study indicate many potential positive social and economic impacts arising from the federalism process. Again, it is important to note that these impacts are inferred as they cannot be easily measured due to the barriers and challenges faced in the implementation of the federal governance systems in Somalia. The inference, however, points to good opportunities for social and economic development in Somalia directly linked to the implementation of a federal system of governance.

The Somali people have very high expectations of the federal system in terms of security, social development, and economic development within the country[217]. This may create challenges for the federalism process as the people expect to see quick solutions in these areas.

Dahiye (2014) noted that federalism was expected to allow negotiated national budgeting and sharing of natural resources as well as national tax revenue benefits leading to equalization of the different regions of Somalia. This would enable the regions to engage in economic development and to provide services to the citizens residing in these regions. As a result, the regions would be able to contribute to the national economy.

As Chevreau (2019) explained, harmonizing federal systems and approaches for resource sharing are likely to formalize and strengthen relationships between the federal member states and the federal government. This would result in broader peace building because the absence of such structures would be economically costly to both the federal government and member states. Relatedly, one key informant observed that federalism provided the space for healthy discussion and consultation on resource sharing between all parties and at all levels.

Another key informant elaborated on social and economic development in Somalia, which has occurred through support provided by development partners through the federalism process. This informant observed that such projects supported by Somali development partners promoted a bottom-up approach and focused on building local institutions and infrastructure and supported the delivery of vital services to local communities. To ensure good federal governance, the support of development partners is needed to enhance institutions and ensure a strong social contract between the government and the people at all levels. Development partners have a supportive role in the federalism process. They ensure that federal government and member-state services are decentralized, and that citizens and communities participate in development decisions

---

[217] Ali, Dahir and Hersi, 2019

that affect them. The development partners avoid concentrating power and resources at a few locations but instead provide balanced, focused support to strengthen governance and humanitarian and social services. Development partners also ensure the support they provide is delivered through political frameworks accepted by all Somali political leaders.

Despite these positive indications, Dahiye's (2014) study argues that federalism is likely to exacerbate the social and regional fragmentation of the Somali state along clan lines, therefore making the task of building a stable and secure country more difficult.

Key informant interviews revealed several changes needed to ensure that federalism leads to positive social and economic impacts. These changes include: (i) putting into place strict rules that outlaw all kinds of social and cultural discrimination and segregation, especially against marginalized and minority groups and that facilitate equal access to government services by all Somalis; (ii) formation of technical teams by the National Consultative Council to guide equitable resource sharing; (iii) undertaking wide-reaching economic and financial reforms to restore fiscal and economic stability through the introduction of an improved financial-management system, improved resource allocation and use, and debt-relief negotiations.

CHAPTER 8

WEAKNESSES *of* FEDERALISM IN SOMALIA *&* REQUIRED REFORMS

8.1. INTRODUCTION

This chapter examines the weaknesses of the federal system in Somalia and identifies necessary reforms for improvement. Five areas of weakness were assessed in the public survey that was administered in six regions of the country. These weaknesses were identified through review of published reports and initial information obtained from focus group discussions and key informant interviews. The five areas include: (i) the lack of a clear definition of the type of federalism practiced in Somalia; (ii) the lack of an effective mechanism to resolve disputes between the federal government and member states; (iii) a lack of capacity and resources on the part of the federal government; (iv) the failure to secure agreement on key issues before federalism was adopted; and (v) a lack of coordination between the member states and the federal government.

These findings provide the foundation for comprehensive analysis and for the development of proposed reforms described in the remaining sections of this chapter. A meticulous examination of each distinct weakness leads to the presentation of strategic solutions specifically crafted to tackle these challenges. The adoption of these targeted reforms is vital not only to strengthen Somalia's federal system but also to enhance its overall effectiveness and ensure its long-term sustainability and resilience.

8.2. GENERAL OVERVIEW OF THE WEAKNESSES OF FEDERALISM IN SOMALIA

When data for all six regions was aggregated and assessed, more than 50% of all respondents were found to agree with the five areas of weakness areas. The lack of capacity and resources on the part of the federal government received highest score (79%), followed by a lack of securing agreement on key issues before adoption of federalism (70%), and then by the lack of a mechanism to resolve disputes between the federal government and member states (68%).

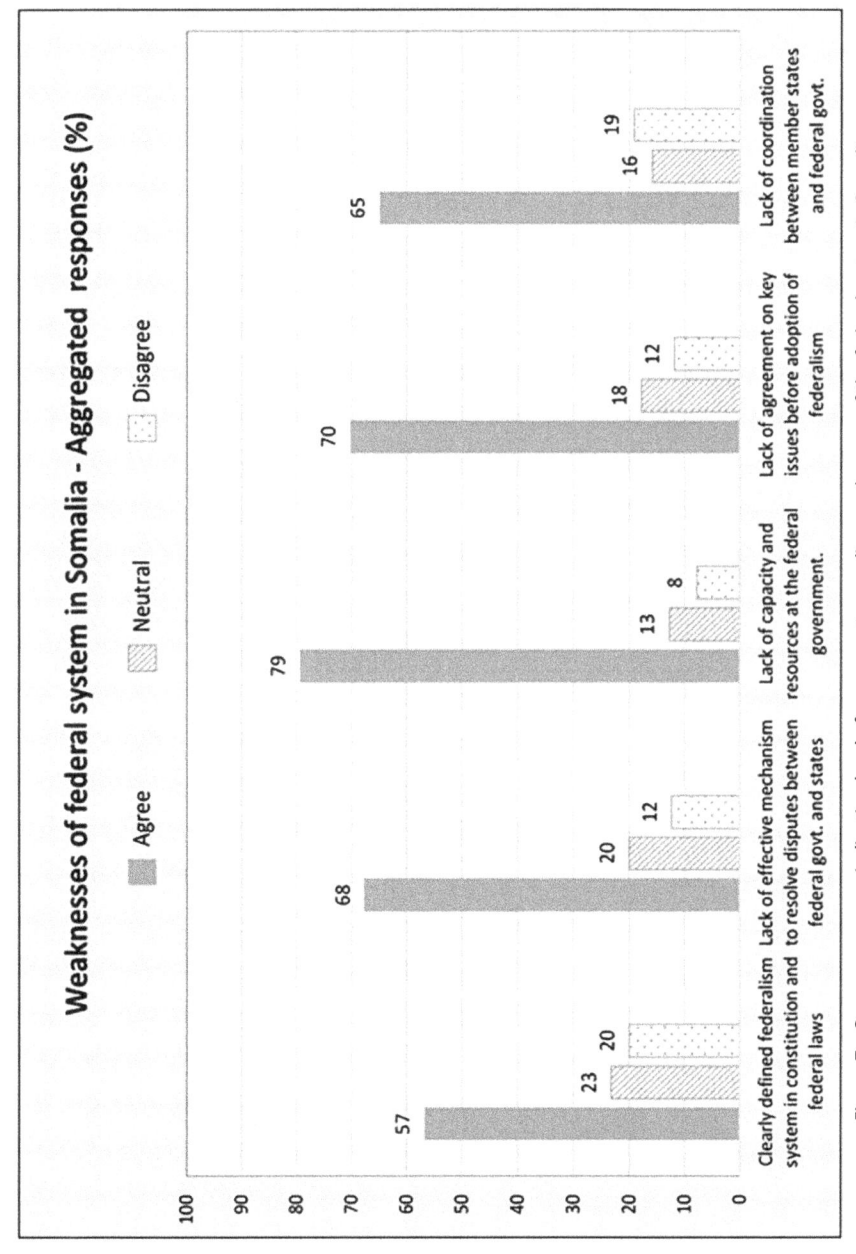

Figure 7 – Survey responses indicating level of agreement regarding weaknesses of the federal system in Somalia.

8.3. LACK OF A CLEAR DEFINITION OF THE TYPE OF FEDERALISM PRACTICED IN SOMALIA

The lack of a clear definition of the type of federal governance system proposed for Somalia has been featured throughout this study and in previous studies.

Ali's (2019) study summarizes the key issues, which include contradictions within the constitution, ambiguities in the federalism process, lack of definition of important elements of the federal system, and omission and neglect of essential issues; all these lead to complications and difficulties with implementation. The omitted items include the division of power and governance, revenue and resource sharing between the federal government and member states, and an electoral model. As Ali notes, the complex nature of Somalia's federal system and the lack of clarity regarding its process have made it difficult to assess its performance or the extent to which it has met the needs of the country. Furthermore, the roles and responsibilities of the federal system are mixed and overlapping; this complicates the federalism process and makes it prone to conflicts between political parties and stakeholders. One key informant agreed with this and observed that the nature and the process of Somalia's federalism remained poorly defined, leading to endless confusion and political instability.

The analysis in this study indicates that the lack of a clear definition of the federal system and of clarity on its process are closely linked to the incompleteness of the provisional constitution. Among the several challenges presented by the provisional constitution are unclear guidelines and technicalities as to how member states should be formed. These have created gaps that lead to tensions between the federal government and aspirant member states regarding such issues as representation of federal member states in the federal judiciary system and to undefined processes, such as constitution review and finalization.

One key informant stated that many attempts have been made to establish different committees to complete the constitution review process, but these efforts have not delivered tangible results and the constitution is still incomplete. This has been a major challenge to the federalism process and remains a key barrier to substantial progress. This weakness indicates that the federal government and member states must work together to complete the review process and finalize the constitution.

8.4. LACK OF AN EFFECTIVE MECHANISM TO RESOLVE DISPUTES

Strong and independent legal institutions with inbuilt mechanisms for resolving disputes are a necessary precondition for the devolution of power or the establishment of a federal governance system. In Somalia, the provisional constitution provides mechanisms for resolving disputes and conflict resolution between the federal government and member states.

As one key informant noted, Article 109 of the provisional constitution provides a mechanism for resolving disputes through the authority of the judiciary. However, disputes and disagreements between the federal government and member states as to the functions of the judiciary system and the institutionalization of its structures have affected the performance of the judiciary.

Respondents in one focus group discussion argued that the weak mechanism for conflict and dispute resolution is combined with the existing political climate, an incomplete constitution, "un-federalized" federal government laws and regulations, and a democratization process paralyzed by the 4.5 clan representative system. Together these influence the development and implementation of a federal system in the country, resulting in common conflicts and disagreements that have weakened government institutions and increased insecurity and lawlessness.

8.5. LACK OF CAPACITY AND RESOURCES FOR THE FEDERAL GOVERNMENT

One key informant informed the study that the federal government has inadequate capacity and resources to effectively implement and manage the federalism process. This limitation is not only in terms of human and financial resources but also in inadequate political control over some of the regions of the country. The capacity and resource limitation could be attributed to the failure of the federal government to establish an efficient mechanism for resource management and distribution across the country. Additionally, the high costs of implementation result in federal member states pursuing their own governance and service delivery systems, placing more strains on the already fragile and resource-scarce system[218].

Further, a key informant reported that day-to-day politicking at all levels of the government took most of the time, leading to inefficiencies and poor use of available resources. For example, three different groups—the Independent Constitutional and Implementation Commission, the Parliamentary Oversight Committee, and the Ministry of Constitution and its federal member-state counterparts—were engaged in the constitution review process; this led to competition and to poor use of available resources. Such situations have limited the federal government's ability to supply enough resources to roll out important components of the federal governance system.

8.6. LACK OF AGREEMENT ON KEY ISSUES DURING ESTABLISHMENT OF THE FEDERAL SYSTEM

Previous studies on federalism in Somalia have argued that, for a country emerging from conflict, any errors at the point of forming and introducing a federal system of governance would have negative impacts, both politically and constitutionally[219]. Unfortunately, as

---

218 Chevreau, 2019
219 Abubakar, 2016

this study highlights, the process of adopting and introducing a federalism system of governance system has generated many difficulties, such as unclear definitions of the federal system and divisive strategies leading to early conflicts among the political groups and local stakeholders. Furthermore, during the writing and adoption of the new provisional constitution, there were disagreements on the process for creating federal member states and for reviewing the constitution.

From the information analyzed by the present study, the key concerns outlined by the stakeholders include: (i) competing interests of regional political leaders and tribal elders; (ii) concerns over fair and transparent formation of the federal member states; (iii) concerns over the constitution review process; (iv) disputes over boundaries of regions and federal member states; (v) limited representation of some Somali groups in the writing and adoption of the provisional constitution; and (vi) the lack of full institutionalization of the judiciary system. These concerns are in line with the findings of Chevreau's (2019) study that, because of the difficulties experienced in the adoption of the federal governance system, the process of implementation was troubled, chaotic, and at times violent. In this setting, the negotiations relating to division of powers and responsibilities between newly emerging federal member states and the federal government were undertaken with deep suspicion and mistrust, especially on the part of the member states.

8.7. LACK OF COORDINATION BETWEEN THE FEDERAL GOVERNMENT AND MEMBER STATES

The poor coordination and cooperation between the federal government and the member states is a major weakness of the federalism process in Somalia. This was clearly stated in the focus group discussions and by key informants in the study. Similar observations were made by previous studies on federalism in Somalia.

The lack of coordination between the federal government and member states takes many dimensions, as identified in the focus group discussions. These dimensions include: (i) federal government laws and regulations that are not "federated" but still aligned to a centralized governance system; (ii) continued influence of the old 4.5 clan representation system that paralyzes democratization and creates political disputes between federal government and member states; (iii) frequent disagreements between the institutions of the federal government and those of the member states leading to increased insecurity and lawlessness; (iv) limited representation of some groups in the constitution process, hence a lack of consensus on the outcomes; (v) difficulties and disputes in the demarcation of member state boundaries; (vi) regional interests and establishment of parallel administrative structure by member states that contradict those of the federal government; (vii) lack of recognition of federal laws by some members states and the issue of declarations of cutting ties with the federal government, which create uncertainty and threaten unity and national cohesion; and (viii) a lack of uniformity in the federalism process where the federal government is seen to favor to some regions or states.

One reason cited for the poor level of coordination and collaboration between the federal government and member states is the weakness in the provisional constitution, which creates ambiguity in the federalism process. Another contributing factor is the lack of genuine agreement between the federal government and member states as to equitable power sharing and to the roles and responsibilities of the different levels of government. A poor national monetary and fiscal system that limits equitable sharing of national resources also contributes to the problem.

8.8. REQUIRED REFORMS

Despite the challenges facing the Somalia federalism process, it is the preferred governance system and has the potential for peace and state building and the capacity to bring about political, social, and economic development in the country. However, this study reveals that the federalism process in Somalia needs to be reformed if it is to address its weaknesses, to become more efficient and effective, and to ensure inclusion, acceptance, and ownership by all parties in Somalia. This section elaborates on these reforms.

Five key areas of reforms within the Somali federal system have been identified by this study. These include: (i) ensuring political inclusion and healthy competition among the different political groups; (ii) ensuring completion of the constitution review and its implementation; (iii) defining clear roles and responsibilities of federal and member state and separation of power between the executive, parliament, and judiciary; (iv) setting up a well-defined and transparent process for the creation of member states; and (v) strengthening federal and state institutions for effective delivery of services. These reforms are briefly summarized below.

8.8.1 Political Inclusion and Healthy Political Competition

To ensure political inclusion and healthy competition, the federal government and member states should work closely together. They should cooperate and coordinate to build plans and frameworks that have clear objectives and timelines and that are aligned with required political, peace-building, and state-building reforms. There is a need to promote healthy political competition by encouraging a multi-party system and moving toward a "one man–one vote" system of elections.

Political inclusion and healthy competition require informing and educating the citizens of Somalia about the importance of federalism as well as its features and requirements. The study reveals a very high level of awareness and acceptance of federalism as the desired governance systems for Somalia but very low understanding of its requirements. Therefore, a nationwide awareness creation and civic education program is required.

Further, to support political development, the federal government, member states, development partners, and all other stakeholders should work together to develop necessary intergovernmental frameworks that support the federalism process in Somalia. Such a framework will ensure that all Somali people, including the minority and marginalized groups, are included in the political-development process and that external support is also delivered within the agreed political framework so that the political determination of the Somali people is not compromised.

8.8.2 Completion and Full Implementation of the Constitution

The success of the federalism process in Somalia is directly linked to a functional constitution that provides all the necessary instruments and provisions for its efficient and effective implementation. Many of the challenges and barriers to the federalism process identified in this study are directly or indirectly related to weaknesses in the provisional constitution.

A previous study on the federalism process[220] argued that the main challenge to the federalism process was the fact that the Somali constitution was still under review, making it difficult to design concrete federal structures and processes that address fundamental issues such as power sharing and constructive political engagement between the federal government and member states. Efforts made to complete the constitution review process were highlighted, but they were noted to be slow and not strongly coordinated, especially between the federal government and the member states.

As urged by key informants, participants of the focus group discussions, and previous studies, the constitution should be the leading tool for guiding the federalism process with every requirement clearly spelled out and without any omission or contradictions. Therefore, for efficient progression of the federalism process, urgent efforts are needed to complete the review of the constitution and then to implement it.

8.8.3 Strengthening the Federal Governance Structure

An efficient federalism governance system in Somalia requires clearly defined roles and responsibilities for the federal government

---

220 Abubakar, 2016

and for member states as well as clear separation of powers. As highlighted in a focus group discussion, there is a need to ensure that the federal government laws and regulation are federated. Currently, most federal government laws and regulations are still aligned to a centralized governance system and do not reflect the current federalism process that is taking place. To support the federal governance system, it is also critical to reform and strengthen the judiciary. This includes strengthening the constitutional court and ensuring it has the capacity to effectively support the implementation of the constitution.

8.8.4 Strengthening Federal and State Institutions for Service Delivery

Weak institutions and poor service delivery at all levels were frequently cited as hindering the federalism process in Somalia. To strengthen institutions and service delivery, there is a need for broad financial reforms across the country, as urged by one key informant. Highlighted reforms include negotiating debt relief, introducing an improved financial management system to restore fiscal and economic stability, and improving aid and grant management and distribution. In this area there is a crucial need to fortify human resources by enhancing training programs, advancing skills development, and improving overall employee wellbeing.

Further, for federalism to progress efficiently, broad-reaching reforms are needed in the security sector. This will provide a conducive and peaceful environment for implementation of the federalism process and the constitution. These reforms need to assess and consider integration of militia into the Somalia National Army and to strengthen the capacity and efficiency of the Somali police force.

CHAPTER 9

CONCLUSION AND PROPOSED FRAMEWORK

9.1. INTRODUCTION

Previous chapters have discussed how Somalia's foray into federalism, against a backdrop of enduring civil conflict and deep-seated political division, exemplifies both the hurdles and the promise of such a system in a setting characterized by pronounced diversity of social and geopolitical positioning and regional specificities. To avoid untenable omissions, attention has been drawn to the divergent opinions and positions about Somalia federalism through a spatial and temporal lens in the context of the decades-long search for a political model that could promote dialogue and rebuild relationships among the fragmented Somali society, establish a governance structure to share power and manage intra-state group conflicts, and ultimately lead to the restoration of Somali nationhood.

But even when we strike common ground that takes into account the historical, social, and political contexts in which Somali federalism was introduced, it is important to remember that not everyone will ascribe to a unified description of Somali federalism. Besides, federal systems evolve with time. This can be seen in Somalia's context when we juxtapose the embryonic stage of Somalia federalism—when the political system was adopted in 2004—with the current manifestation of the federal arrangement with its full-fledged membership of five federal member states, the Banadir region, the emerging administration in Sool, Sanaag and Cayn–Khatumo territories, and Somaliland.

However, we can go beyond the historical and political implications of the system and rationalize the intellectual content and the transformative effects of Somalia's federalism that has generated so much interest in and debates about national government, sovereignty, identity, and the benefits and challenges of various forms and concepts of political systems.

Today there is a growing tendency to equate federalism with notions of autonomy at the local level and with unity and power sharing at the national level; this makes the federal political system a strategic compromise that is more palatable than the undesirable alternatives of state failure, centralism, and secessionism. It suggests that the discourse has shifted away from the contesting narratives about its origins and the selection of federalism as an appropriate political model for Somalia to impassioned and somehow less enlightened arguments about *the type of federalism that is suitable for* Somalia.

This does not, however, mean that federalism, while entrenched in Somalia's Provisional Federal Constitution, has become part of the country's quotidian political existence. At the outset federalism was known to be a complex and multi-dimensional governance model offering a rich tapestry of sociopolitical dynamics that could be used to profoundly shape national identity, promote unity, and ensure a fair allocation of power and resources. However, the architects of Somalia's federalism left significant aspects of the federal structure to be hammered out through political negotiations among the center and peripheries and through the process of reviewing and completing the provisional constitution. There are convincing arguments that the constitutional review and the final settlement on jurisdictional, administrative, and fiscal arrangements must take place in tandem. But we must be mindful that the provisional constitution, while it is the supreme law of the land, is not the panacea for the multifactorial challenges of Somalia federalism, nor are political agreements and structural reforms without strong institutions and mechanisms to resolve disagreements and foster cooperation.

Somali federalism is at a critical juncture. The risk is high that regressive political decisions, which run counter to the federal ideals, can set the country further back into more political pluralization and perpetual crisis, resulting in the forfeiture of the normative achievements of the last twelve years. That is why we need to illuminate these risks, giving fresh impetus to the discursive construction of Somali federalism as a pragmatic response to Somalia's social and political divisions.

This concluding chapter endeavors to accomplish two interlinked but separate tasks. First it summarizes the analysis, encapsulating the core insights and providing critical perspectives as part of the global discourse on federalism, particularly relevant to post-conflict environments and the distinctive African political milieu. Second, it articulates the trajectory of Somali federalism and makes recommendations on shaping and adapting the federal system to Somalia's context and on cultivating a culture of democratic institution building and a learning process that can ameliorate the current model in this epochal moment of Somali state building. The second task will be addressed in a contextually relevant, forward-looking, and practical framework tailored to Somalia and its federal experience. This framework, derived from comprehensive research data and enriched by comparisons with other federal structures, particularly in African states with analogous socio-cultural and economic backdrops, must be seen as more than a mere set of guidelines. It is also an opportunity to reflect the changing contours of Somalia's political landscape and to offer a dynamic, evolving strategy that invites continual engagement, thoughtful dialogue, and creative adaptation.

9.2. SUMMARY OF ANALYSIS

9.2.1 Importance of the Federal Governance System

Federalism is an important governance system and power-sharing mechanism. It is practiced in countries where 40% of the world's population resides. This number is even greater, more than 70%, when you consider countries that employ other elements of decentralized governance. Federalism, however, is not only a governance system; it has many other sociopolitical benefits that are appurtenances of national identity and loyalty, self-preservation, inter-state collaboration, and the equitable distribution of resources, among others.

Six African countries are considered to have federal systems of government— Comoros, Nigeria, South Africa, Ethiopia, Sudan, and Somalia—but few research studies have been carried out on African federal systems. From the wider global experience, successful federalism is underpinned by strong and democratic rule-of-law institutions, but is contingent upon the prevailing local political, social, and economic conditions in each society: hence the need to study how these factors influence federalism in specific countries.

Federalism in post-conflict settings and in Africa has not been sufficiently studied. This research study aimed to elucidate Somali federalism and its trappings to inform and guide its effective implementation in Somalia, to contribute to available knowledge, and to stimulate new thinking on federalism in post-conflict settings and in the African context. The study has built on existing research on federalism, especially in Somalia since its onset in 2004, but also in other countries. Therefore it highlights challenges and potentials and identifies lessons and best practices from countries with similar cultural, social, economic, and environmental contexts.

9.2.2 Federalism Process in Somalia

The federal governance system and process in Somalia, with all its challenges, has become an important tool for political and socioeconomic development. The federal governance system was advocated in Somalia as a means for peace and a contrivance for state building after prolonged civil strife. It was seen as an alternative mechanism for sharing national resources and as possibly the only practical way to unite the nation while accommodating its regional, social, cultural, political, and economic differences.

Somalia, like many other African countries, has struggled to build a unified country after gaining independence from colonial rule.

However, the overthrow of the Said Barre regime led to prolonged civil war and political struggle. Following failed efforts to unite the nation, Somali political leaders agreed to and legally approved a federal system of governance in 2004 setting in motion the process of establishing federal member states. The ultimate goal of federalism was to build a sustainable, smoothly running, and effective governance system where federal and member-state levels of government collaborate effectively for peace, the efficient use of resources, and social and economic development throughout the country while providing equal social, political, and economic representation for all people, including minorities and marginalized groups.

9.2.3 Factors Shaping Federalism in Somalia

Seven factors were identified as having either positive or negative effects on federalism in Somalia: (i) federalism deals with political division and mistrust; (ii) federalism is hampered by weak institutions and resource constraints; (iii) federalism is promoted by peaceful regions; (iv) federalism helps overcome national fragmentation; (v) federalism accommodates all parties and groups; (vi) federalism is favored by Somali people who have strong affiliation with their region; and (vii) improved development in some Somali regions following the fall of unitary governance favors federalism.

The study assessed these factors and revealed that the Somali people agree with six of the seven factors. The one factor where there was no agreement related to federalism's ability to accommodate all parties, including diverse ethnic and cultural groups and their differences.

The Banadir region stood out from the other five areas evaluated in the study. Among those surveyed in Banadir, clear consensus or dissent emerged on only one of the factors influencing federalism: the preference for federalism among those with strong regional affiliations. Notably, this was the only factor on which there was unanimous agreement across all six regions surveyed.

The study discovered that federalism has the potential to overcome the division and mistrust caused by prolonged political instability, insecurity, and civil strife. Doing so, however, requires healthy relationships between the federal government and the federal member states, balanced power and resource sharing, real reconciliation efforts across Somalia to heal past wounds, and efforts to address contradictions in the provisional constitution to support effective implementation of the federalism governance system.

Weak institutions and resource constraints negatively affect implementation of federalism in Somalia in many ways. These include weak controls on the federalism process that minimize the influence of external partners, limit the capacity of institutions responsible to implement the federalism process, and make it difficult for key institutions and stakeholders to collaborate and coordinate effectively. This weakness is also reflected in the poor definition and understanding of Somalia federalism and its expected outcomes and in the slow progression leading to limited results.

The argument that federalism is a suitable governance system for Somalia is strongly supported by experiences in regions of Somalia such as Puntland and "Somaliland" that have successfully practiced some form of subnational governance for a long time. It is also supported by the fact that four federal member states—Galmudug, Hirshabelle, Southwest, and Jubaland—have been formed successfully and are operational now. This is a testimony to the assertion that adopting this governance concept delivers peace and state-building dividends.

Efforts to promote peace and political development have presented federalism as a solution to bring back unity in Somalia after the entrenched mistrust and division caused by the civil war. Federalism is also seen as a system that provides a solution to mitigate the concentration of power in the hands of the few, as was the case with the previous dictatorial regime that perpetrated abusive actions and suppressive policies. However, the Somali federalism process has faced many challenges while simultaneously continuing to evolve and mature. Innovative solutions such as the formation of the National Leadership Forum (NLF) to address implementation difficulties have played important roles.

The Somali people recognize various factors shaping federalism and see it as a system designed to meet the needs of all clans, rather than as a framework to include every group and party, particularly those defined by cultural differences. Somali people have observed the past political reality as one where the political majority correlated to a clan-based demographic majority and where cultural patriotism was emphasized. The federalism process should find frameworks that will move away from this past to an era of emphasis on national stability.

Somali people are inclined toward local development in their regions of origin and toward promotion of decentralization of political power to the different regions of the country. Both leaders and citizens see the federal governance system as the best method to share power and wealth fairly across Somalia. They see giving the member states and their local level governance structures more autonomy to being the solution to retaining a degree of influence at the local level.

9.2.4 Tools and Instruments Guiding Federalism in Somalia

The study assessed seven tools and instruments important in guiding federalism in Somalia. These include: (i) the provisional constitution; (ii) laws and regulations of the federal government; (iii) intergovernmental frameworks; (iv) laws and mechanisms for transferring funds; (v) harmonized monetary and fiscal policies; (vi) roles and responsibilities of the federal government and member states, and (vii) laws and regulations of member states aligned to federal government plans and priorities.

Overall, the provisional constitution and the roles and responsibilities of the federal government and member states were recorded as having a higher level of importance among the tools and instruments guiding federalism in Somalia.

In the six areas surveyed, a significant number of respondents—between 20% and 28% of those surveyed—recorded "neutral" or "no opinion" responses to the questions regarding the tools and instruments guiding federalism in Somalia. These percentages may indicate a low level of awareness among the Somali people regarding these tools and instruments.

As a federalism instrument, the provisional constitution has, to some degree, positively reoriented Somalia's politics from violent conflict between political groups and communities to peaceful political dialogue, engagement, collaboration, and partnership. However, the implementation of the provisional constitution has presented many challenges that require innovation, learning, and ongoing review. The federal government and member states have the opportunity to address existing and emerging challenges through the work of the Independent Constitutional Commission and the Parliamentary Constitutional Oversight Committee and to learn from the experiences and practices of federal governance systems in other countries.

Federal laws and regulations are important in guiding federalism in Somalia. They help define and provide direction to the federalism process, support healthy collaboration between the federal government and member states, and ensure inclusion and equal representation of all parties, including minorities.

However, the federal laws and regulations are not fully in line with the legislative and jurisdictional processes and practices of federalism. The study identified several needed improvements. These include: (i) ensuring federal laws and regulations are fully "federalized"; (ii) completing the review of provisional constitution review and its ratification; (iii) formation of the constitutional court and transformation to democratic "one person–one vote" elections; (iv) review and delineation of the roles and responsibilities between the federal government and federal member states; (v) initiation of a nationwide civic education program to create awareness about the federalism process; and (vi) development of intergovernmental frameworks to support efficient collaboration and coordination with all parties and stakeholders.

Intergovernmental cooperative frameworks play an important role in guiding and supporting the federalism process. The key frameworks identified by the study include the National Consultative Council (NCC) and the Mutual Accountability Framework. While the implementation of these frameworks is supported by Somali development partners, there is room for improvement to ensure that technical, advisory, and financial support is provided through an agreed-upon political framework. This support should not concentrate power and resources in a few areas but should distribute them equally to strengthen the governance of member states as well as social and humanitarian services.

The study revealed that in addition to the existing cooperative frameworks, a parallel and broader technical and policy framework is required alongside the federalism process to strengthen institutional capacity and service delivery mechanisms. This will support the existing intergovernmental frameworks and allow equal opportunity to all regions. It will transform the federalism process, making it more meaningful and tangible to all Somali people. It will articulate and harmonize the roles and responsibilities of the federal government, federal member states, local governments at the district level, and all other parties and stakeholders.

Harmonized monetary and fiscal policies are critical for federalism in Somalia. Disputes concerning fiscal management have limited its progression. The constitution and other federal laws need to consider and articulate monetary and fiscal issues clearly. Proposed improvements include: (i) negotiating debt relief; (ii) restoring fiscal and economic stability by improving the financial-management system; (iii) establishing consistent financial regulations across the country to mitigate disputes regarding the allocation of resources between federal government and member states and at the local government level; and (iv) improving management of grants and aid.

Clear roles and responsibilities for both the federal government and the member states are important for moving the federalism process forward. They are also needed for transitioning Somalia's federalism process from one dominated largely by the political elite and prone to disagreement to one that is efficient with healthy engagement at all levels of governance. Improvements needed include clearly defined powers and responsibilities of the federal government and the member states and the development of a parallel but broad policy framework that articulates and harmonizes subsidiary issues related to roles and responsibilities of different parties, institutions, and stakeholders.

For federalism to be efficient, member states' laws and regulation need to complement and be aligned with those of the federal government—but this is not the current practice. Instead, harmonizing the laws and regulations of member states with the plans and priorities of the federal government is compromised by a number of challenges, including: (i) inconsistency among the member states in the formulation of laws and regulation and in application of the federal laws; (ii) member states' operations that antagonize the federal government; (iii) breaches of some articles of the constitution by member states; (iv) inadequate cooperation of member states with the federal government where member states take up roles reserved for the federal government; (v) member states pursing their own governance and service delivery systems leading to higher costs; (vi) limited and weak mechanisms for resource assessment and redistribution across the country; (vii) federal laws, regulations and plans that have not been subjected to the appropriate consultation and development processes; (viii) federal laws and regulations, such as those concerned with basic service delivery, that infringe on the competencies of the member states; (ix) federal laws and regulations that have been passed but that require political agreement of the member states; and (x) centralized institutions, reminiscent of the old dictatorial regime, which are not compatible with the federalism process.

The federal government and member states have taken steps to address these challenges. One example is the established of the National Leadership Forum, which among other achievements, has created ways to harmonize the federal government and member-state systems and strengthen relationships between the two levels of government.

9.2.5 Awareness of Federalism and Its Impact on Development

The study has assessed the Somali people's awareness of federalism in two broad areas: their awareness of federalism as a governance system, and their preferences as to how power is shared between the federal government and member states.

The study revealed that the Somali people have a high level of awareness of federalism. They identify it as the most suitable governance system for Somalia when it is compared to decentralized or unitary systems. Their reasons for preferring federalism include political stability, better service delivery, economic development, good governance, equitable power sharing, and prevention of dictatorial rule.

Despite the significant awareness and support for federalism as the preferred governance system, the Somali people have expressed limited understanding of its intricate features and of how it functions. There is a need for nationwide civic education campaigns to inform and educate the people on the different aspects of federalism and their practical implication.

Published studies confirm the Somali people's awareness of federalism but observe that the federal system of governance is still very young. It faces many barriers, and its details are yet to be fully understood by the people. This is expected, considering that federalism has replaced a centralized and clan-based power-sharing system that existed for nearly three decades.

While power-sharing preferences vary greatly within and among the regions of Somalia, the highest levels of consensus were found in Galmudug and Hirshabelle, followed by Jubaland and Puntland.

The Somali people prefer that the federal government controls foreign affairs, national defense, monetary matters, immigration and border control, and planning and international cooperation. In addition to the clear preferences indicated by respondents in the public survey and in information obtained from desk reviews, key informant interviews and focus group discussions suggested that people favor having member states manage local tax collection, social affairs, and initiatives aimed at poverty reduction. The people prefer that member states control local tax collection, social affairs, and areas related to poverty reduction. They prefer concurrent power sharing between the federal government and member states in the areas of policing, environmental protection, development of state-level infrastructure, and commerce.

The study assessed the impact of federalism on development in two areas: political development and socioeconomic development. Introduction of a federal governance system in Somalia has led to substantial political development with consistent progress in establishing a healthy political environment for peace and state building. Political gains have included: (i) endorsement of a provisional constitution; (ii) establishment of four member states and their local institutions; (iii) establishment of constitutional affairs ministries at federal and member-state levels; (iv) establishment of the upper house of parliament to represent the interest of member states; and (v) establishment of several commissions to facilitate preparation, negotiation, and implementation of federal governance policies and legal frameworks. These commissions include the Boundaries and Federation Commission, the National Leadership Forum, the National Consultative Council, and the Independent Constitutional Review and Implementation Commission.

Despite these positive political impacts, the prevailing political environment limits the performance and effectiveness of the federal governance system and its mandated institutions and commissions. Three key areas need to be addressed to remove these constraints; they include the completion of the constitution review process, agreement on the structure of the member states, and consensus on power and resource sharing and distribution.

The federalism process has had many potentially positive social and economic impacts, although these are difficult to quantify currently due primarily to a lack of reliable data on many sectors. However, federalism requires a negotiated and equitable distribution of the national budget and of the benefits from natural resources and tax revenues. This arrangement fosters equal social and economic development across all regions of the country.

For federalism to sustain consistent social and economic development, local institutions should be strengthened, and strong social contracts should be made with the people by the federal, member-state, and local levels of government. Services provided by the federal government and member states should be decentralized. Citizens and local communities should be involved in planning and implementing development decisions. Power should not be concentrated at a few locations, and governance, social, and humanitarian services should be improved. Further, Somalia's development partners have an important role in the federalism process, but their support should be delivered through political frameworks agreed upon by all Somali political leaders.

Several improvements are needed to ensure federalism leads to social and economic development. These include: (i) putting into place strict rules that outlaw all types of social and cultural discrimination and segregation, especially against marginalized and minority groups, and that facilitate equal access to government services for all people; (ii) forming technical teams by the National Consultative Council to guide equitable resource sharing; (iii) undertaking wide-reaching economic and financial-management reforms through introduction of improved financial management systems and restoration of fiscal and economic stability; (iv) improving grant and aid coordination and allocation; and (v) initiating and engaging in debt-relief negotiations.

9.2.6 Weakness of Federalism and Required Reforms

The study identified and assessed five areas of weakness in the federal governance system established in Somalia. These include: (i) a lack of a clear definition of the type of federalism practiced in Somalia; (ii) a lack of an effective mechanism to resolve disputes between the federal government and member states; (iii) limited capacity and resources at the federal level; (iv) a lack of agreement on key issues prior to the adoption of federalism; and (v) a lack of co-ordination between the member states and the federal government.

The study found all five areas of weakness to be important, but the most significant weaknesses were the limited capacity and resources by the federal government, the lack of agreement on key issues prior to adoption of federalism, and the lack of a mechanism to resolve disputes between the federal government and member states.

A lack of clarity on the federalism system introduced in Somalia led to implementation difficulties and made it impossible to assess the performance of federalism. There are no benchmarks or indicators of inputs and outputs to evaluate how well federalism is meeting the needs of Somalia. The lack of clarity is seen in: (i) the contradictions within the constitution; (ii) the ambiguities in the federalism process; (iii) the lack of definition of important elements of the federal system; and (iv) the omission of details on essential issues such as power sharing and division of power, revenue, and resource sharing between the federal government and member states, and on an electoral model.

The study further found that the lack of clarity regarding Somalia's federalism system is, in many ways, linked to the incomplete constitution. The constitution does not provide clear guidelines on: (i) how member states should be formed and how to deal with related technical issues; (ii) representation of federal member states in the federal judiciary system; and (iii) processes for completing the constitution. While all these issues present barriers to progress in the implementation of federalism, the more concerning is the fact that the protracted constitutional review process has so far not delivered any meaningful results. The federal government and member states should work together to fast-track the review process and finalize the constitution.

Despite the mechanisms created by the provisional constitution to resolve disputes between the federal government and members states, disagreements on the functions of the judiciary and on the institutionalization of its structures have limited this dispute mechanism, which relies on the judiciary. This arrangement has been compromised further by the existing political environment, by an incomplete constitution, by "un-federalized" federal government laws and regulations, and by a democratization process that is partly paralyzed by the 4.5 clan representative system. Overall, the lack of an effective system for dispute resolution has limited the implementation of federalism in the country.

The study revealed that the federal government has inadequate capacity and resources to effectively implement and manage the federalism process. These deficits can be attributed to several factors: the federal government's failure to establish an efficient resource management and distribution mechanism, high implementation costs associated with federalism, an excessive focus on politics, and a duplication of roles between the federal government and member states, which resulted in the wastage of limited resources.

Lack of agreement on key issues prior to the establishment of the federal governance system has led to an implementation process that is troubled, chaotic, and sometimes violent. The study found that some of the issues and concerns creating disagreement have stemmed from differences relating to the following: (i) interests of regional political leaders and tribal elders; (ii) fair and transparent formation of the federal member states; (iii) the constitution review process;

(iv) regional and federal member-state boundaries; (v) limited representation of some Somali groups in the writing and adoption of the provisional constitution; and (vi) institutionalization of the judiciary system.

The poor coordination between the federal government and member states is a major weakness in the federalism process in Somalia. It is caused primarily by disagreements and differences between the federal government and member states stemming from: (i) "un-federated" federal government laws and regulations; (ii) continued influence of the 4.5 clan representation system; (iii) disagreements between institutions of the federal government and those of member states; (iv) limited representation of some groups in the constitution process; (v) disputes in the demarcation of member-state boundaries; (vi) establishment of parallel administrative structures by member states; (vii) lack of recognition of federal government laws by some members states; (viii) negative messages about the federal government from member states due to perceived concentration of power; (viii) lack of uniformity in the federal government's dealings with member states; and (ix) sharing of humanitarian and development aid.

Despite the challenges that the Somalia federalism process faces, it is the preferred governance system and has the potential for peace and state building. It also has the capacity to bring about political, social, and economic development in the country. Reform of Somalia's federalism process is needed to address its weaknesses, to make it more efficient and effective, and to ensure inclusion, acceptance, and ownership by all parties in Somalia.

The study identified five key areas of reforms and action within the Somali federal process. These include: (i) ensuring political inclusion and healthy competition among the different political groups; (ii) ensuring completion of the constitution review process and its implementation; (iii) defining clear roles and responsibilities between the federal government and federal member states and separating powers between the executive, parliament, and the judiciary; (iv) establishing a well-defined and transparent process for creating member states; and (v) strengthening federal and state institutions for effective service delivery.

To ensure political inclusion and healthy competition, the federal government and members states should work together to: (i) build plans and frameworks that have clear objectives and timelines; (ii) promote healthy political competition by encouraging a multiparty system and a "one person–one vote" system; (iii) organize a nationwide campaign to raise awareness and provide civic education on federalism and its implications; and (iv) work with Somalia's international partners to develop and implement intergovernmental frameworks that support the federalism process and that ensure all Somali people and groups are represented in the political development and that external support is delivered within an agreed-upon political framework that secures the interests of the Somali people.

The success of the federalism process in Somalia is directly linked to a functional constitution that provides all the necessary instruments and provisions for its efficient and effective implementation. Many of the challenges and barriers to the federalism process are directly or indirectly linked to the incomplete provisional constitution. Efficient progression of the federalism process requires that the constitution review be completed and the constitution implemented.

An efficient federalism governance system in Somalia requires clearly defined roles and responsibilities for the federal government and for member states as well as a clear separation of powers. Federal laws and regulations should be designed and applied with a federalist approach, and the judiciary should be reformed and strengthened to ensure it has the capacity to effectively support the implementation of the constitution and the federalism process.

Weak institutions and poor service delivery at all levels are cited as hindering the federalism process in Somalia. To strengthen institutions and service delivery, there is a need for: (i) broad financial reforms across the country, including negotiation of debt relief, the introduction of an improved financial-management system to restore fiscal and economic stability as well as improvement in aid and grant management and distribution; (ii) human resources improvement through training, improving terms of service, and removing ghost workers from payrolls by using technology such as biometric systems; and (iii) broad-reaching security reforms, including integrating militia groups in the national army and strengthening the national police force.

9.3. PROPOSED FRAMEWORK

There is a compelling case for change in Somalia regarding federalism, not only in the need to adapt its principles but also in the need to operationalize federal arrangements. These arrangements include collaboration between the levels of government and the sharing of resources.

This section develops a framework that can provide guidance and serve as a tool to evaluate the key elements and steps for the structuring, implementation, and institutionalization of federalism in Somalia. This framework should be used to stimulate debate on the purpose and principles of federalism in Somalia and on how the implementation of this political system could be adapted to our unique historical, social, and political circumstances. The framework contains twelve domains particularly suited to the context of Somalia. To make this framework non-prescriptive, it is necessary to describe both what is required and how these perform within the framework.

Somali Federal Governance Implementation Framework

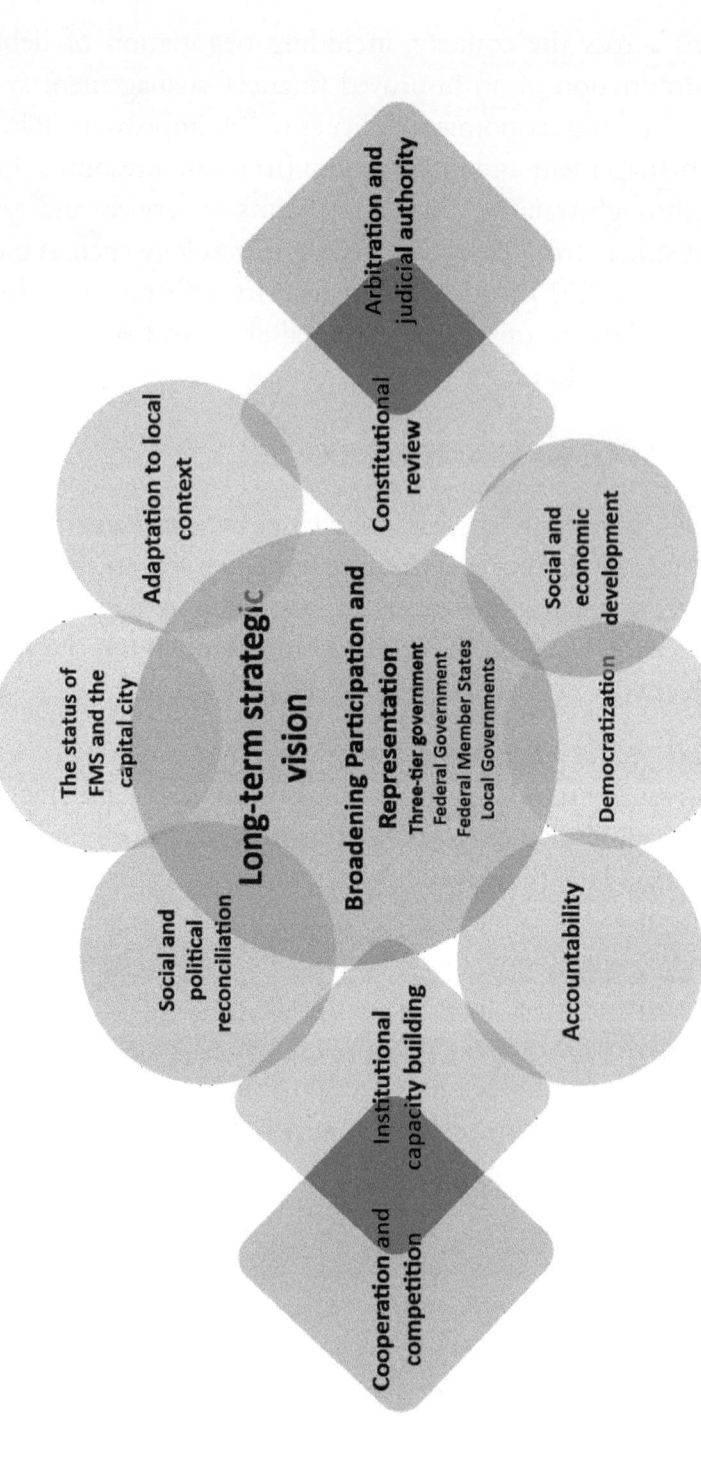

Figure 8. Implementation framework for federalization in Somalia

9.3.1 Developing a Long-term Strategic Vision for Somali Federalism

It is difficult to implement federalism without establishing and agreeing to a set of principles that flow from the foundational character of federalism. Such principles can guide the process, during both the negotiations and the implementation of any agreement reached. These principles include the recognition that federalism is a system of *two or more levels of government that none is subordinate to the other*. Under federalism, sovereignty is shared, the resolutions of autonomy and unity are prescribed by the constitution, and there are reciprocal relations and cooperation between the levels of government, horizontally and vertically.

Any long-term vision for reform and fully implemented federalism in Somalia must start with the establishment of ground rules for **negotiations in good faith, genuine political commitment**, and **unity of purpose**. The declaration of the political commitment could be made at a high-level national constituent conference where the guiding principles, implementation pathways, and timelines for the federalization implementation process are outlined.

The concept of "negotiation in good faith" does not mean sidestepping the challenging aspects of state building or avoiding issues related to power and resource sharing. Neither does it imply ignoring disagreements over fundamental principles or pressing issues in the federalization of Somalia. It means a commitment to negotiate for the benefit of all Somali people, states, and different levels of the government. It means to move away from the status quo, stalemates, and the zero-sum thinking that have plighted Somali politics in the last two decades.

Since federal political systems are organized in different forms in theory and practice, the strategic vision must define what Somali federalism will look like. It must accommodate those who advocate for an established hierarchy of powers, subordination, clearly defined spheres and exclusionary decision-making at the top. It must also accommodate those who believe in federalism as based on pragmatism, bargaining, compromise, and consensus. This vision must address the exercise of power and the allocation of resources as topics to be negotiated and given at the level that is the most suitable and relevant. It is particularly important for the vision to deal with "the elephant in the room," the perpetual scramble for power and resources in the guise of dividing responsibilities for the levels of government. It is easy to identify and delineate a set of powers for each of the different levels of government to ensure the social and political legitimacy of these polities. In practice, however, very few functions can be assigned and managed solely at a specific tier in the different levels of government. The vision must therefore articulate mechanisms to promote cooperative arrangements and address emerging issues of subsidiary federalism, spillover effects and trade-offs, and effective machinery to resolve disagreements. This framework, therefore, recommends a strategic vision based on the promotion of a collaborative approach to build a strong central government and strong federal member states through a democratic federal system.

9.3.2 Broadening Participation and Representation

It is apparent that some deficiencies in the discussions and efforts to implement federalism in Somalia are related to the limited engagement and involvement of large sections of Somali society. Since 2012 the key actors in the negotiations on the federal structure and the review of the provisional constitution have been limited to the political elites in the federal government and federal member states. There is a need to shift Somalia' federalization process from one largely dominated by political elites and prone to disagreements to one with healthy engagement by all stakeholders at all levels. The role of local governments, civil society organizations, academia, women, and youth groups is of paramount importance. Full engagement not only brings knowledge, different perspectives, and different experiences to the discussions but it also promotes equity, inclusivity, and a culture of consultation, collaboration, and participatory decision-making. Participation has been reduced because the work of the federalization in Somalia has been led by departments with limited capacity and experience within the ministries of interior of the federal government and the federal member states. The provisional constitution created a Boundaries and Federation Commission but this important body has never been properly implemented. There are few other forums for federalization at the national level or in the states.

This framework proposes to establish an independent "federation commission" at the national level as well as subnational commissions at the member-state level to further develop and improve the implementation outcome of Somali federalism. The present Boundaries Commission should be assigned only to resolve issues involving disputes over administrative and jurisdictional issues between states. These commissions should be part of the negotiating process and should help the levels of government work out solutions based on principles of federalism and in the spirit of collaboration and compromise.

Another specific participation conundrum is related to our understanding of representation at the national level. The House of the People is composed of representatives from communities in the member states. The upper house was designed to represent the interests and priorities of the federal member states themselves. One can argue that the opinions of the member states are represented at the national level within the bicameral legislature. But there is a different perception of representation on the part of people who serve at the national level. Irrespective of where they are from, they will be categorized as "the federal government." They will advance the interests of the center and will be inclined to support the concentration of power in the center, as is justified in the quest for a strong central government. This contradiction could have been resolved through the democratization of the representation process in one person–one vote universal suffrage. Since Somalia's federal government was built around power-sharing arrangements between the

Somali clans in the 4.5 formula, it is hard to fathom to whom these representatives are accountable.

The most significant benefit of federalism is the decentralization of governance to the local level. This increases citizens' participation in decision-making, planning, and prioritizing of services and in the way services are delivered. The framework proposes a shift from the current form of federalism that is engrossed in a tug-of-war between the federal government and governments of the federal member states. It recognizes the role of local governments as the third tier in the principles and structure of federalism in Somalia. No one can deny that it is important to have certain matters decided locally by lower levels of government; these matters include identifying needs, planning and delivering social services, and providing education, health and sanitation, culture and sports. By transferring powers and resources to the local governments, the two higher tiers can swiftly empower the districts, municipalities, and village councils to bring together budgets and public services, plan and propose investment in local areas, and involve a wider range of community members to tackle local challenges. Whereas intergovernmental relations are important for collaboration between the federal level and federal member states, interlocal government cooperation between districts and municipalities and interdepartmental relations between various departments within and across the federal government and federal member states is critical for strengthening federalism and bringing services closer to communities.

9.3.3 Adapting Federalism to the Somali Context

The lack of definition for the type of federalism that Somalia has adopted is being used as an argument to create ambivalence about and invoke opposition to federalism in Somalia. This argument seeks to discredit the significant progress that has been made toward peace building and state building through this cooperative process. However there must be a paradigm shift in the status quo of the present Somali federalism, which is focused narrowly on the restoration of Somalia nationhood—on bringing together federalism.

There must also be an embrace of cooperative federalism in which federal principles, modalities, practices, and institutions are legalized, institutionalized, and realized.

I have given examples of types of federalism in different contexts and countries. These examples illustrate the importance of historical, social, and political contexts, of the role of governance and judicial cultures in shaping the type of federalism appropriate to these countries. Somalia is no different. Instead of such arguments as "We do not even know which type of federalism we have adopted," we must ask more cogent questions: Which type of federalism is applicable? Which circumstances are so unique in Somalia's experience that we must choose one type over another?

I have compared the different forms of federalism of a selected number of countries to illustrate the effects of context and sociopolitical circumstances on the type of federalism these countries practice. It is evident that there is no one-size-fits-all type of federalism, but the strength of federalism lies in its adaptability and ability to evolve over time. Our arguments, therefore, must reflect these realities and focus on the more important questions of how we can place the different powers, responsibilities, and resources in the most suitable level of government, including in local governments. We must determine how we can use the federal principles to carve out and adapt our own federal structure. How can we best fulfill the aspirations of the Somali people for local autonomy that prioritizes better local services on one side and inclusion and sharing of power and resources at the national level? It is possible that we will arrive at our unique federal system and one day call it "Somali federalism."

I have the view that, at these initial stages of Somali federalism, the need for bargaining, collaboration, and compromise is far greater than any imperative for a clearer separation of powers and functions. Additionally, it is easy to recommend the cooperative types of federalism—such as Canada's or South Africa's—in theory, but it is undeniable that other models, such as those of the United States or

Germany, have their own merits and could be effectively explored in the Somali context.

The study's findings have revealed that many Somalis support the provisional constitution's power-sharing arrangements, such as those for foreign affairs, national defense, monetary matters, and immigration and border control; these should be used as the starting point for negotiations. Many service delivery and functional assignments—such as local tax collection, the social affairs of education and health, and poverty reduction programs—are seen as the remit the federal member states. Concurrent power sharing between the federal government and member states is preferred in policing, environmental protection, the planning and development of state-level infrastructure, and commerce. This framework proposes to adapt a type of federalism that ensures a set of competencies for the levels of governments like those defined in the provisional constitution but with provisions to ensure collaboration, co-decision-making, and intergovernmental relationships between the center and the states.

9.3.4 Building Institutional Capacity

Key reforms and capacity building for government institutions in both levels is essential to make the federalism process efficient, effective, and results-oriented. No single entity in the Somali federal structure will make any progress in state building without collective action to organize and install solutions to correct the inherent institutional weakness and the legacy of state failure. The key institutions involved in the federalism process should be provided with sufficient financial and human resources as well as technical and functional capacities; these are necessary to embed federalism in the social, cultural, political, and governance structures and to create the necessary enabling environment for active engagement and collaboration between all stakeholders. Such institutions include the ministries of interiors at the federal and member-state levels, the independent commissions for federalism and resolution of boundary disputes, the federal judicial organs, and the intergovernmental relations units.

9.3.5 Constitutional Review and the Implementation of Federalism

There is a risk of the country sliding back into further division and political stalemate due to the ongoing controversies and disagreements over the federal government's unilateral review and amendment process of the Provisional Federal Constitution. The review process must enjoy the support of all sides—the national government, the member states, and the different communities. Priority should be given to the review of all contentious provisions that require political agreement between the federal government, federal member states, and other stakeholders. Technical committees should be set up to facilitate dialogue, to inform and guide negotiations, and ultimately to reach joint agreement on these issues. The extent to which the jurisdictional authorities of the center and the states are clearly defined in the constitution should be negotiated and agreed. The next phase of the constitutional review should focus on harmonizing the Provisional Federal Constitution and the constitutions of the federal member states and preparing a national referendum on the final draft of the constitution.

9.3.6 Arbitration and Judicial Authority

The incessant squabbling and disagreements between the federal government and member states do not only reveal constitutional and structural problems in Somalia federalism. These are the clear manifestation of the lack of mechanisms for independent arbitration, judicial authority, and enforcement of the constitutional, jurisdictional, and sovereignty rights of the two levels of the government. This framework puts the constitutional court at the heart of the implementation process for both the constitution and Somali federalism. Therefore, the formation and operation of the constitutional court must be expedited so the interjurisdictional disputes and spillovers can be resolved through legal means. Non-judicial entities such as the proposed federation commission and the Boundaries Commission should play significant roles in resolving disputes between the levels of government.

9.3.7 Cooperation and Competition

In federal political systems, competition for power and resources between the center and the states and among the states is inevitable. Federalism in Somalia has created new fora for political competition. It is the ideal model to solve the zero-sum and winner-takes-all culture that became pervasive during the conflict. Cooperation among the levels of government is necessary since certain responsibilities overlap extensively. At the same time, healthy competition must be encouraged to produce innovative and responsive services to meet the needs of the communities. The balance of cooperation and competition can be managed through the intergovernmental relations mechanism established by the provisional constitution, but this instrument has only occasionally been used to reach agreement on aspects of resource sharing.

Competition between the federal government and member states for the meager local resources is relatively low. The most glaring adversarial competition between these entities at present is the allocation of foreign aid. Humanitarian and development assistance profoundly influence the conduct of both levels of the Somalia government. There are several bones of contention regarding allocation of foreign aid and the extent to which external actors influence the standing, legitimacy, and authority of the different levels of government; this is part of the wider debate on the governance of international aid and on how program-funding decisions are made.

The political proviso and negative implications of legitimizing one level with donor funds has demonstrable effects in Somalia. Channeling donor funds through the federal government without an accountability framework that ensures member-state representation and inclusive decision-making could provide the center with ammunition to further undermine the authority, legitimacy, and ability of the states to provide public goods and may have destabilizing effects. Dealing directly with the member states has similar adverse effects and could place resources into the hands of state political leaders who would benefit more from the fragmentation of the nation than from collaboration and compromise. That is why the allocation of foreign aid should not disturb the level playing field in Somalia but should play a part in institutionalizing and enforcing a culture of co-operation and co-decision-making.

This framework proposes the operationalization and institutionalization of intergovernmental relations under the office of the prime minister as stipulated by the Provisional Federal Constitution. The agreements reached in this intergovernmental relations forum must be legalized through the respective federal and state parliaments.

9.3.8 Accountability

One can question the separation of accountability in this section from the participatory implementation of federalism or from the institutional-capacity building described above. This is done to emphasize the interdependence of government levels and the necessity of making them accountable to citizens through constitutional, legislative, and democratic processes. Additionally, this section addresses the impact of democratization on the implementation of Somali federalism.

Accountability takes different forms and procedures for individual government officials, offices, departments, and even for the government as a whole. We must establish and strengthen accountability policies, procedures, instruments, and practices in all levels of government. The most straightforward accountability arrangement should reinforce the separation of power between the three branches of the federal and state governments. Participatory policy-making and decision-making between the federal government and federal member states through intergovernmental relations could promote accountability and mutual respect for explicitly defined responsibilities of different levels of governments and for their shared role in the federal governance of Somalia. Other effective accountability tools include the free media, civil society organizations, and the business community.

This framework proposes four domains for accountability to the intergovernmental relations that comprise the most relevant structure for implementing federalism in Somalia: i) engagement and representation of relevant levels of government in the horizontal and vertical intergovernmental interactions to increase plurality of actors and cooperation; ii) coordination of intergovernmental engagements, meetings, and programs across the federal government and federal member states by an impartial intergovernmental relations secretariat; iii) use of effective communication channels to build trust between levels of government, promote active engagement and consultation, support better governance, and improve policies and services; and iv) consensus as a means of reaching decisions and agreements in layered compromises negotiated and assessed at various stages for the common good.

9.3.9 Democratization

Democracy and federalism should be viewed through the same lens and favored as appropriate models for increasing representation and participation. In the Somali context, these are effective ways to resolve tribal-based power and resource-sharing conundrums.

This framework provides the basic ingredients of democratic transformation of Somali federalism. The first ingredient focuses on the participatory policy-making requirement in the formulation of laws and policies governing democratization. Both levels of government in Somalia federal governance are guilty of violating the most basic principle of democracy: citizens' involvement in discussions about their political governance, including the laws and policies used to govern them. A simplified and practical electoral law is needed, one that contains measures to cultivate and strengthen a culture of democracy. Such a law should not arbitrarily limit citizens' rights to political participation or formation of parties. The current electoral laws in Somalia are regressive, prescribing the existence of only three parties in any given timeframe and limiting the creation of new political associations to once every ten years.

The second required ingredient is independent, impartial, and politically neutral electoral commissions at both the federal and federal-state member levels. These should be complemented by an independent judiciary that upholds the rule of law and ensures fair adjudication of disputes, thereby safeguarding democratic processes.

Democratization cannot be implemented without good local governance at the village, district, and regional levels. Civil society organizations, free media, academia, and other supporting democratic governance structures and institutions—such as community committees for basic social services—are all vital for democracy. Equally important are strict rules that outlaw all kinds of social, political, and cultural discrimination and segregation, especially against marginalized and minority groups, and interventions to facilitate equal access to political participation and government services by all people.

9.3.10 The Status of Federal Member States and the Capital City

Federalization of Somalia is an ongoing and evolving process. The rules and regulations about the number and size of the constituent units should be reviewed and negotiated. Article 49, Clause (6) of the current provisional constitution states that "[b]ased on a voluntary decision, two or more regions may merge to form a Federal Member State"[221]. The formation of new federal member states has faced challenges due to this constitutional provision. One state, Galmudug, was formed in 2006 and did not meet the above criteria but was later recognized by the federal government in 2015. The federal government and member states should therefore review and revise the process, laws, and policies for the formation and status of federal member states and for the national capital, Mogadishu.

9.3.11 Social and Economic Development

Federalism, as a governance approach for setting priorities at the local level, presents a real opportunity for social and economic devel-

---

221 PFC, 2012: 14

opment for all regions of Somalia. The prospect of local policy-making in social and economic programs offers huge dividends in delivering better social services and fostering economic growth. Again, spurring economic growth involves intergovernmental cooperation, assigning fiscal authority, and equitable resource sharing at the local, state, and national levels.

Intergovernmental relations will be a vital mechanism to undertake wide-reaching economic and financial-management reforms through the introduction of improved financial-management systems and restoration of fiscal and economic stability. As described above, federal grants and coordination and allocation of foreign aid are effective tools to ensure collaboration and compliance between the center and the states. The levels of government should work together and define clearly the social and economic programs and infrastructure projects that are purely local and those that are regional or national in scope. The vibrant private sector and civil society groups should be encouraged through progressive policies to participate in the planning and delivery of social services and economic growth and development.

9.3.12 Social and Political Reconciliation in the Implementation of Federalism

Social reconciliation has not been given enough attention in the context of federalism in Somalia. Efforts to reconcile the existing divisions within Somali society and to address the enduring impacts of five decades of military dictatorship and civil war have been insufficient. The complex history of inter-clan conflict within Somali society and the collective nature of the violence has made it difficult to individualize victims and perpetrators. Because there are victims and perpetrators in each clan, the issue of reconciliation must be centered on granting forgiveness, particularly on the concept of "Xalay Dhaley (forgiving past grievances and starting a new)," on paying compensation in rural areas, and on sharing political power between rival clans at the national level. The ongoing disputes over land and property, particularly in the inner cities, keep alive the dark legacy of the civil war.

Attaining peace and stability is not possible when relations and trust between these formerly antagonistic clans are still weak. Fear and mistrust have not been eradicated, and the terms of agreements are not adhered to. It is important to acknowledge that all reconciliation processes require meaningful and stable conflict-resolution mechanisms and enabling political, social, and institutional structures.

On the political side, the current unhealthy relationship between the two levels of government is the main barrier to state building. In particular, it is a barrier to implementing the federal structure, strengthening the rule-of-law institutions, and transitioning to democracy. In other words, the lack of political agreement on the most contentious issues regarding power and resource sharing, and concerns of alternative institutional designs and constitutional amendments that might deviate from the agreed federal structure, have complicated and frustrated the implementation of federalism in Somalia.

This framework proposes a social reconciliation model that combines Somali community-based "traditional" justice ("Xeer") and restorative justice. It calls for the establishment of a national reconciliation commission to develop reconciliation processes and post-conflict justice mechanisms that include the strengthening of the formal justice system to promote accountability in the future.

REFERENCES

Aalen, L. (2006). Ethnic federalism and self-determination for nationalities in a semi-authoritarian state: The case of Ethiopia. *International Journal on Minority and Group Rights* 13(2/3): 243–261.

Abbink, J. (2006). Discomfiture of democracy? The 2005 election crisis in Ethiopia and its aftermath. *African Affairs* 105(419): 173–199.

Abdi, F. (2024). *Relational Leadership and Governing: Somali Clan Cultural Leadership.* The Journal of Social Encounters: Vol. 8: Iss. 1, 154-173.

Abdullahi, A. (2020). Somali elite political culture: Conceptions, structures, and historical evolution. *Journal for Somali Studies* 5: 30-92.

Abubakar, M. A. (2016). The patterns of state rebuilding and federalism in Somalia. *African Journal of Political Science and International Relations* 10(6): 89–95.

Adam, H. (1992). Somalia: Militarism, warlordism or democracy? *Review of African Political Economy*, 19(54): 11–26.

Adebanwi, W., Obadare, E. & Diamond L. J. (2013). *Democracy and Prebendalism in Nigeria: Critical Interpretations*. Palgrave Macmillan.

Ahmed, A. H. (2014). Constitution-making in Somalia: A Critical Analysis, 1960 – 2013. University of Nairobi.

Ali, Y. S. A., Dahir, A. H., & Hersi, Z. D., (2019). *Federalism in post-conflict states: Assessing Somalia's challenges and the way forward.* Perspectives on Federalism, 11(2): 56–63.

Amnesty International. (1992). *Somalia: A Human Rights Disaster*. Amnesty International.

Anderson, G. (2008). *Federalism: An Introduction*. Oxford University Press.

Arretche, M. (2019). *Paths of Inequality in Brazil: A Half-Century of Changes*. Springer.

Bataveljić, D. (2012). Federalism: The concept, development and future. *International Journal of Humanities and Social Science* 2(24): 21–31.

Battuta, I. (1975). *Ibn Battuta in Black Africa* (Trans: Said Hamdun and Noel King). Rex Collings.

Benz, A., & Broschek, J., Eds. (2013). *Federal Dynamics: Continuity, Change, and the Varieties of Federalism*. Oxford University Press.

Birmingham, D. (1995). *The Decolonization of Africa*. Routledge.

Birkland, T. A. (2008). Is federalism the reason for policy failure in Hurricane Katrina? *Publius: The Journal of Federalism* 38 (4): 692–714.

Boadway, R. & Shah, A. (Eds.) (2007). *Intergovernmental Fiscal Transfers: Principles and Practice*. R. Boadway. & A. Shah (Eds.) Public Sector Governance and Accountability Series. The World Bank.

Boadway, R. & Shah, A. (2009). *Fiscal Federalism: Principles and Practice of Multiorder Governance*. Cambridge University Press.

Bose, S. (2002). *Bosnia after Dayton: Nationalist Partition and International Intervention*. Oxford University Press.

Brown D. J. L. (1956). *The Ethiopia-Somaliland Frontier Dispute*. International and Comparative Law Quarterly. 5(2):245-264.

Burgess, M. (2006). *Comparative Federalism: Theory and Practice*. Routledge.

References

Burgess, M. (2012). Federalism in Africa, an essay on the impacts of cultural diversity, development and democracy. *The Federal Idea.* https://docplayer.net/24010025-Federalism-in-africa-an-essay-on-the-impacts-of-cultural-diversity-development-and-democracy.html.

Busse, R., & Blümel, M. (2014). Germany: Health system review. *Health Systems in Transition* 16(2), 1–296.

Cassanelli, L. (1982). *The Shaping of Somali Society: Reconstructing the History of Pastoral People, 1500–1900.* University of Philadelphia Press.

Chabal, P. & Daloz, J-P. (1999). *Africa Works: Disorder as Political Instrument.* Indiana University Press.

Chandler, D. (2000). *Bosnia: Faking Democracy after Dayton.* Pluto Press.

Chemerinsky, E. (2023). *Constitutional Law: Principles and Policies*, 7th ed. Aspen Publishers.

Chevreau, O. M., (2019). Federalism and Post-Conflict State Building: The case of Somalia (master's thesis, Univ. of Bradford), http://hdl.handle.net/10454/17441.

Clapham, C. (1985). *Third World Politics: An Introduction.* University of Wisconsin Press.

Collier, P. (2003). Ethnicity, politics and economic performance. *Economics and Politics* 12(3): 225–245. https://onlinelibrary.wiley.com/doi/abs/10.1111/1468-0343.00076.

Connell, R. (2007). *Southern Theory: The Global Dynamics of Knowledge in Social Science.* Routledge.

Cooper, F. (2002). *Africa Since 1940: The Past of the Present.* Cambridge University Press.

Cotran, E. (1963). Legal problems arising out of the formation of the Somali Republic. *International and Comparative Law Quarterly* 12: 1010–1026.

Courson, E. (2009). *Movement for the Emancipation of the Niger Delta*. Nordiska Afrika Institute.

Dafflon, B. (2002). *Local Public Finance in Europe: Balancing the Budget and Controlling Debt*. Studies in Fiscal Federalism and State-local Finance Series. Edward Elgar Publishing.

Dahal, D. R & Bhatta, C.D. (2008). *The Relevance of Local Conflict Resolution Mechanisms for Systematic Conflict Transformation in Nepal*. Berghof Foundation for Peace Support.

Dahiye, M. I. H., (2014). *Federalism and National Stability: The Case of Somalia 1999–2013*. University of Nairobi.

Daniel, T. (2007). *The Architecture of Government: Rethinking Political Decentralization*. Cambridge University Press.

Davidson, B. (1975). *Somalia: Towards Socialism*. Race & Class, 17(1), 19-37.

Dawisha, A. (2009). *Iraq: A Political History from Independence to Occupation*. Princeton University Press.

De Waal, A. (2000). *Who Fights? Who Cares? War and Humanitarian Action in Africa*. Africa World Press.

Deschouwer, K. (2009). *The Politics of Belgium: Governing a Divided Society*. Palgrave Macmillan.

Detterbeck, K. (2005). *Cartel Parties in Western Europe?* Sage Publications. doi: 10.1177/1354068805049738.

Drysdale, J. (2001). *Whatever Happened to Somalia?* Haan.

Ekeh, P. P. (1975). Colonialism and the two publics in Africa. *Comparative Studies in Society and History*, 17(1)): 91–112.

References

Elazar, D. J. (1984). *American Federalism: A View from the States.* Harper & Row.

Elazar, D. J. (1987). *Exploring Federalism*. University of Alabama Press.

Elmi, A., & Barise, A. (2006). *The Somali conflict: Root causes, obstacles, and peace building strategies.* African Security Review, 15(1): 32–54. doi:10.1080/10246029.2006.9627386.

Eno, M.A. and Eno, M., 2007. *Inclusive but Unequal: The Enigma of the 14th SNRC and the Four-Point-Five (4.5) Factor.* In Ed. Osman, A. A. and Souaré, I. K. *Somalia at the Crossroad: Challenges and Perspectives on Reconstituting a Failed State.* London: Adonis & Abbey Publishers Ltd, pp.58-80.

Erk, J. (2014). Federalism and decentralization in Sub-Saharan Africa: Five patterns of evolution. *Journal of African Affairs*, 24(5): 535–552. doi.org/10.1080/13597566.2014.971769.

Falleti, T. G. (2010). *Decentralization and Subnational Politics in Latin America*. Cambridge University Press.

Federal Republic of Nigeria (1999). Constitution of the Federal Republic of Nigeria.

Federal Republic of Somalia (2012). The Somalia Provisional Constitution.

Feeley, M. & Rubin, E. (2011). *Federalism: Political Identity and Tragic Compromise*. University of Michigan Press.

Fessha, Y. (2010). *Ethnic Diversity and Federalism: Constitution Making in South Africa and Ethiopia*. Routledge.

Fitzgibbon, L. (1982). *The Betrayal of the Somalis*. Rex Collings.

Fleiner-Gerster, T., Misic, A. & Töpperwien, N. (2005). Swiss Constitutional Law. Kluwer Law International.

Fombad, C. M. (2018). Constitutional entrenchment of decentralization in Africa: An overview of trends and tendencies. *Journal of African Law* 62(2): 175–199.

Foucaoult, M. (2007). *Security, Territory, Population: Lectures at the Collège de France, 1977–78.* Palgrave Macmillan.

Fukuyama, F. (2004). *State-Building: Governance and World Order in the 21st Century*. Cornell University Press.

Galbraith, P. (2007). *The End of Iraq: How American Incompetence Created a War Without End.* Simon & Schuster.

Gazibo, M. (2013). Beyond electoral democracy: Foreign aid and the challenge of deepening democracy in Benin. WIDER Working Paper Series, World Institute for Development Economic Research.

Ghai, Y. & Galli, G. 2006. *Constitution Building Processes and Democratization*. International Institute for Democracy and Electoral Assistance.

Goldsmith, S. & Crawford, S. (2014). *The Responsive City: Engaging Communities through Data-Smart Governance*. Jossey-Bass.

Griffiths, A., Chattopadhyay, R., Light, J. & Stieren, C. (2020). *The Forum of Federations Handbook of Federal Countries*. Springer.

Hardin, R. (2013). Why a Constitution? In D. Galligan & M. Versteeg (Eds.), *Social and Political Foundations of Constitutions* (pp. 51–72). Comparative Constitutional Law and Policy. Cambridge University Press.

Henrard, K. (2000). *Devising an Adequate System of Minority Protection*. Brill-Nijhoff.

Hess, R. L. (1966). *Italian Colonialism in Somalia*. University of Chicago Press.

References

Hills, R. M. (2006). Federalism as Westphalian liberalism. *Fordham Law Review* 75(2): 16.

Hochstetler, K. (2000). Democratizing pressures from below? Social movements in the new Brazilian democracy. In Kingstone, P. and Power, T. J. (eds), *Democratic Brazil: Actors, Institutions, and Processes* (pp 167–184). University of Pittsburgh Press.

Hoehne, M. and Luling, V. (2010). *Peace and Milk, Drought and War—Somali Culture, Society and Politics*. Hurst & Company.

Hogg, P. W (1985). *Constitutional Law of Canada*. Carswell Publishers.

Hueglin, T. & Fenna, A. (2015). *Comparative Federalism: A Systematic Inquiry*. University of Toronto Press.

Jakab, A., Dyevre, A. & Itzcovich, G. (2017). *Comparative Constitutional Reasoning*. Cambridge University Press. doi.org/10.1017/9781316084281.

Jeffery, C. (1999). *Recasting German Federalism: The Legacies of Unification*. Bloomsbury.

Johnson, D. H. (2003). *The Root Causes of Sudan's Civil Wars*. The International Africa Institute and Indiana University Press.

Jorre, J. de. St. (1972). *The Nigerian Civil War*. Hodder and Stoughton.

Kapil, R. L. (1966). *Integrating Disparate Colonial Legacies: The Somali Experience*. Race, 8(1), 75-88.

Kefale A. (2013). *Federalism and Ethnic Conflict in Ethiopia: A Comparative Regional Study*. Routledge.

Keil, S. & Anderson, P (2018). Decentralization as a tool for conflict resolution. In K. Detterbeck & E. Hepburn (Eds.) *Handbook of Territorial Politics* (pp. 89–104). Edward Elgar.

Kimenyi, M. S. (2017). *Devolution and Development: Governance Prospects in Decentralizing States*. Routledge.

Kingdon, J. (1995). *Agendas, Alternatives and Public Policies*, 2nd ed. Harper Collins.

Klay, A. M. A. (2015). *Federal Somalia: Not If But How*. (Policy brief.) Heritage Institute for Policy Studies.

LaSelva, S.V. (1996). *The Moral Foundations of Canadian Federalism: Paradoxes, Achievements, and Tragedies of Nationhood*. McGill-Queen's University Press.

Laitin, D. (1976). The political economy of military rule in Somalia. *Journal of Modern African Studies* 14(3): 449–468.

Laitin, D. (1979). The war in the Ogaden: Implications for Siyad's role in Somali history. *Journal of Modern African Studies* 17: 95–115.

Laitin, D., & Samatar, S. (1987). *Somalia: Nation in Search of a State*. Gower Publishing.

Lemarchand, R. (1972). Political clientelism and ethnicity in tropical Africa: Competing solidarities in nation-building. *American Political Science Review* 66(3): 68.

Lewis, I. (1988). *A Modern History of Somalia: Nation and State in the Horn of Africa*. Westview Press.

Lewis, I. (2003). *A Modern History of the Somali: Nation and State in the Horn of Africa*. Ohio University Press.

Lewis I. M. (2004). *Visible and Invisible Differences: The Somali Paradox*. Africa, 74(4):489-515.

Lewis, I. (1961). *A pastoral Democracy*. Oxford University Press.

Lewis, I. (1980). *A Modern History of Somalia: Nation and State in the Horn of Africa*. Longman.

References

Linder, W. (1994). *Swiss Democracy: Possible Solutions to Conflict in Multicultural Societies*. Macmillan.

MacCormick, N. (1995). The Maastricht-Urteil: Sovereignty now. *European Law Journal* (1):259–266.

Mamdani, M. (2018). *Citizen and Subject: Contemporary Africa and the Legacy of Late Colonialism*. Princeton University Press.

Manor, J. (1999). *The Political Economy of Democratic Decentralization*. World Bank.

Marchildon, G. P. & Allin, S. (2021). *Health Systems in Transition: Canada*. 3rd ed. University of Toronto Press.

Marshfield, J. (2011). *Federalism and political competition in emerging democracies.* Washington University Global Studies Law Review 10(2).

Martinez-Vazquez, J. & Alm, J., (Eds.) (2003). *Public Finance in Developing and Transitional Countries: Essays in Honor of Richard M. Bird*. Edward Elgar.

Menkhaus, K. (2018). *Elite bargains and political deals project: Somalia case study.* DFID Stabilisation Unit.

Miller, A. S., (1983). Toward a definition of "the" Constitution. *University of Dayton Law Review* 8(3): 633–712.

Mohamed, M. & Mosley, J. (2014). *On Federalism and Constitutionality in Somalia: Difficulties of "Post-transitional" Institution Building Remains*. African Arguments.

Mohiuddin, G. & Islam, M. (2016). *Decision Style in Islam: A study of Superiority of Shura (Participative Management) and Examples from Early Era of Islam*. European Journal of Business and Management.

Mosley, J. (2015). *Somalia's Federal Future: Layered Agendas, Risks and Opportunities.* Chatham House.

Mukhtar, M. H. 1989. The emergence and the role of political parties in the inter-riverine region of Somalia from 1947 to 1960 (Independence). *Ufahamu: A Journal of African Studies* 17(2): 57–69.

Mustapha, A. R., & Whitfield, L., (Eds.) (2009). *Turning Points in African Democracy*. Boydell and Brewer.

Nkrumah, K. (1960). "Ghana's republic is born." Quoted in Rothchild, D. (1966). The limits of federalism: An examination of political institutional transfer in Africa, *Journal of Modern African Studies* 4(3): 275–293.

O'Leary, B. (2009). *How to Get Out of Iraq with Integrity*. University of Pennsylvania Press.

O'Toole, L. (1993). *American Intergovernmental Relations: Foundations, Perspectives, and Issues*. CQ Press.

Oates, W.E. (1999). An essay on fiscal federalism. *Journal of Economic Literature*, 37(3): 1120–1149.

Paine, J. (2019). *Ethnic Violence in Africa*. Cambridge University Press.

Panagariya, A., Chakraborty, P. & Rao, G. M. (2014). *State-Level Reforms, Growth, and Development in Indian States*. Oxford University Press.

Payton, G. (1980). The Somali coup of 1969: The case of Soviet complicity. *Journal of Modern African Studies*, 18: 493–508.

Perry, V. (2015). Constitutional reform in Bosnia and Herzegovina: Does the road to confederation go through the EU? *International Peacekeeping* 22: 490–510.

Peterson, B. & Zaki, M. (2023). *Reforming Somali Customary Justice: Pathways to Adapting Xeer Procedures and Practices*. Sababi Institute.

Peterson, P. E. (2010). *Saving Schools: From Horace Mann to Virtual Learning*. Harvard University Press.

Peterson, P. E. (1995). *The Price of Federalism*. Brookings Institution.

PFC (2012). See Federal Republic of Somalia. (2012). The Somalia Provisional Constitution.

Prunier, G. (1997). *The Rwanda Crisis: History of a Genocide*. Columbia University Press.

Putnam, D. B. & Noor, M. C. (1993). The Somalis: Their History and Culture, CAL Refugee Fact Sheet Series, No. 9. Refugee Service Center. Eric Document ED377254.

Qur'an. Tarsir Ibn Kathir - English (2003). Darusslam Publications.

Rao, M. G., & Singh, N. (2006). *The Political Economy of Federalism in India*. Oxford University Press.

Reuchamps, M. (2015). *Minority Nations in Multinational Federations: A Comparative Study of Quebec and Wallonia*. Routledge.

Riker, W. H. (1964). *Federalism: Origin, Operation, Significance*. Little, Brown and Company.

Rothchild, D. (1966). The limits of federalism: An examination of political institutional transfer in Africa, Journal of Modern African Studies, 4(3): 275–293.

Sahih Muslim, English (2007). *The Book on Governance, Hadith 1855a*. Darusslam Publications.

Samatar, A. (1988). *Socialist Somalia: Rhetoric and Reality?* Zed.

Samatar, A. (1997). Leadership and ethnicity in the making of African state models. *Third World Quarterly* 18: 687–707.

Samatar, A., & Samatar, A. (2008). *Africa's First Democrats: Premier Abdirizak H. Hussein and President Aden A. Osman*. Bildhaan: International Journal of Somali Studies 2: 1–64.

Samuels, D. (2003). *Ambition, Federalism, and Legislative Politics in Brazil*. Cambridge University Press.

Sathe, S. P. (2003). *Judicial Activism in India: Transgressing Borders and Enforcing Limits*. Oxford University Press.

Schapiro, R. (2007). Federalism as Intersystemic Governance: Legitimacy in a Post-Westphalian Word. 57 Emory L.J.

Smoke, P. (2003). Decentralization in Africa: Goals, dimensions, myths and challenges. *Public Administration and Development* 23(1): 7–16.

Solomon, P. H. (2004). Judicial power in Russia: Through the prism of administrative justice. *Law and Society Review* 38(3): 549–582.

Stepan, A. (1999). Federalism and democracy: Beyond the U.S. model. *Journal of Democracy* 10(4): 19–34.

Steytler, N. & Mettler, J. (2001). Federal arrangements as a peacemaking device during South Africa's transition to democracy. *Publius* 31(4): 93–106.

Steytler, N. (Ed.) (2005). *The Place and Role of Local Government in Federal Systems*. Konrad-Adenauer-Stiftung.

Steytler, N. (2017). *The Constitutional Court of South Africa: Reinforcing an Hourglass System of Multi-Level Government*. University of Toronto.

Stoner-Weiss, K. (2006). *Resisting the State: Reform and Retrenchment in Post-Soviet Russia*. Cambridge University Press.

Suberu, R. (2001). *Federalism and Ethnic Conflict in Nigeria*. United States Institute of Peace Press.

References

Swenden, W. (2006). *Federalism and Regionalism in Western Europe: A Comparative and Thematic Analysis*. Palgrave Macmillan.

Taylor, M. (2008). *Judging Policy: Courts and Policy Reform in Democratic Brazil*. Stanford University Press.

Turton, D. (2006). *Ethnic Federalism: The Ethiopian Experience in Comparative Perspective*. Addis Ababa University Press.

Umbach, M. (2002). *German Federalism: Past, Present, Future*. Palgrave.

United Nations General Assembly (UNGA). (1949). Questions of the Disposal of the Former Italian Colonies. A/Res/289.

Vaughn, S. (2003). "Ethnicity and Power in Ethiopia." (PhD diss. University of Edinburgh).

Watts, R. (2008). *Comparing Federal Systems*, 3rd ed. Montreal & Kingston, London, Ithaca: McGill-Queen's University Press.

Wheare, K. C. (1946). *Federal Government*. Oxford University Press.

Young, C. (1997). *The African Colonial State in Comparative Perspective*. Yale University Press.

Young, J. (1996). Ethnicity and power in Ethiopia. *Review of African Political Economy* 23(70): 531–542.

Zhuravskaya, E. (2000). Incentives to provide local public goods: Fiscal federalism, Russian style. *Journal of Public Economics* 76(3): 337–368.

INDEX

A

A Challenging Transition, xv
Abdirashid Ali Shamarke, 97
Abdullahi Isse, 89
Abubakar, 100, 124, 131, 132, 134, 140, 154, 155, 166, 170, 207
Abuja, 11
Abyssinia, 86
Aden Abdullahi Osman Daar, 97
Aden Abdulle Osman, 89
Afgoye, 86
Africa, vi, xxviii, xxxi, 10, 56, 57, 58, 59, 60, 61, 62, 63, 66, 70, 71, 75, 76, 78, 108, 177, 208, 209, 210, 211, 212, 213, 214, 215, 216, 217, 218
African, x, xx, xxiii, xxiv, xxv, xxvii, 1, 56, 57, 58, 59, 60, 63, 64, 68, 76, 77, 78, 79, 93, 108, 126, 176, 177, 207, 211, 212, 214, 215, 216, 217, 219
African Union, 63, 126
African Union Mission, 126
Alberta, 47
Amazon, 36
American, 44, 211, 212, 214, 216
Amhara, 68
Amharas, 70
Anderson and Keil, 19, 21, 97
Arab, 12, 85, 86
Arab and Persian, 85
Arab Emirates, 12
Arta, xix, 92
Arta Conference, 92
Articles of Confederation, 9
Asho Ali Mohamoud, xi
Australia, 10, 13, 51
Australian Capital Territory, 10

B

Baghdad, 42
Banadir, xix, xxviii, xxix, 112, 121, 123, 125, 130, 139, 144, 146, 152, 154, 174, 178
Banadir Regional Administration, xxix
Baraawe, 85
Barawe, 87
Bargal and Alula, 86
Barre, iv, x, 91, 92
Basic Law, 30
Bavaria, 46
Belgian, 33, 70
Belgium, v, 10, 32, 34, 35, 210
Berbera, 85, 87
Berlin, 11
Biafran War, 37, 57
Bosnia and Herzegovina, 10, 40, 41, 42, 43, 216
Bosniaks and Croats, 40
Bosnian War, 40
Boundaries and Federation Commission, 156, 185
Brandenburg, 46
Brazil, v, 10, 36, 38, 39, 49, 51, 53, 208, 213, 218, 219

221

Brazilian, 36, 38, 213
Brčko District, 40
Britain, 87, 88
British, iv, 30, 87, 88, 89, 94, 96
British and Italian, 94
British Foreign Secretary Ernest Bevin, 87
British North America Act, 30
British Protectorate, 89
British Somaliland, 87
Brussels, 10
Bundesrat, 30

C

Cabinet, 12
California and Texas, 46
Cameroon, 59
Canada, v, 11, 18, 29, 31, 32, 49, 213, 215
Canada and Germany, 49
Canadian, 30, 44, 214
Capital District, 12
Case of Somalia, x, xv, xxiv, xxv, xxvii, 210
Cassanelli, 87, 88, 89, 91, 209
Chattopadhyay, 10, 212
Chevreau, 15, 16, 17, 18, 19, 100, 123, 124, 130, 142, 143, 148, 151, 156, 158, 166, 209
Citizen Constitution, 36
Citizenship, 114
City of Buenos Aires, 10
Comoros, 11, 60, 177
Conflict Africa, x, xv, xxiv, xxv, xxvii
Constitution, 34, 71, 81, 84, 107, 108, 110, 112, 116, 170, 185, 199, 207, 211, 212, 215

Constitutional Court, 110, 218
Constitutional Dilemmas, 101
COVID, 30

D

Dahal and Bhatta, 19
Dahir, 123, 129, 130, 145, 146, 147, 158, 207
Dahiye, 124, 129, 132, 142, 152, 158, 210
Darod, 92, 128
Darwish, 114
Dayton Peace Accords, 40
DC, 12
Derg, 40
Diaspora, 130
Digil, 92, 94, 97, 129
Digil and Mirifle, 94, 129
Division of Powers, 7
Djibouti, xix, xxviii, 87, 92, 96
Dr. Abdiweli M. Ali Gas, xiii, xv
Dr. Guled Salah Barre, iii, iv, xvi, xvii, xix, xx, xxi
Dr. Kwame Nkrumah, 59
Dr. Nkrumah, 59
Drysdale, 91, 210
Dynamics and Federalism, 101

E

Eastern Cape and Limpopo, 74
Egypt, 85
Egyptian, 85
Egyptians, 85, 86
Elazar, 5, 8, 13, 18, 48, 73, 211
Ethiopia, vi, xxviii, 11, 40, 42, 43, 60, 62, 64, 66, 71, 75, 76, 77, 86, 87, 89, 91, 96, 97, 177, 207, 208, 211, 213, 219

Ethiopia and Nigeria, 77
Ethiopia and South Africa, 62
Ethiopian, 41, 61, 72, 88, 219
Ethiopians, 87
EU, 8, 216
Europe, 9, 210, 219
European, 8, 24, 30, 58, 86, 87, 96, 97, 215
European Union, 8, 24
Europeans, 96, 97

F

Federal Constitutional Court, 31
Federal Dependencies, 12
Federal Government, vii, viii, xxiii, xxviii, 5, 109, 110, 112, 114, 115, 123, 219
Federal Government of Somalia, xxiii, 110
Federal Government of Somalia (FGS), 110
Federal Member States of Somalia, 110, 112, 114, 115, 116, 117, 203
Federal National Council, 12
Federal Parliament, 116
Federal Republic of Nigeria, 72, 211
Federal Republic of Somalia, 110, 111, 211, 217
Federal Supreme Council, 12
Federal Supreme Court, 34
Federalism, v, vi, vii, viii, x, xv, xx, xxvii, 6, 7, 9, 15, 21, 23, 29, 32, 36, 40, 50, 63, 65, 66, 67, 69, 103, 104, 106, 120, 123, 125, 176, 177, 178, 179, 180, 184, 187, 193, 196, 199, 200, 203, 204, 207, 208, 209, 210, 211, 213, 215, 217, 218, 219
Federalism Imperative, x, xxvii
Federation of Bosnia and Herzegovina, 40, 41
FGD, 124, 125, 129
FGDs, xxviii, xxix, 120, 123, 125, 137
FGS, 113, 114, 115, 116, 117
FGS. The FGS, 114
Finance Commission, 34
Fiscal federalism, 23, 31, 36, 43, 219
Flemish, 10, 33, 70
Flemish and Wallonia, 10
Flemish and Walloon, 33
FMS, 111, 112, 113, 114, 115, 116, 117
FMS. Article, 111
Fombad, 108, 212
Foreign, 114, 212
Foucaoult, 107, 212
French, 87, 96
French Somaliland, 87
Fukuyama, 60, 212
Furthermore, xx, xxx, 22, 62, 113, 125, 129, 148, 155, 164, 167

G

Galgaduud, 112
Galmudug, xxviii, 99, 112, 121, 129, 130, 133, 139, 140, 142, 144, 146, 147, 152, 154, 155, 179, 185, 203
Galmudug and Hirshabelle, 152, 185
Garowe I, 129
Gauteng, 62, 74

Gauteng and Western Cape, 74
Gedo, 127
General Siyad Barre, 90
German, 30, 51, 213, 219
Germany, v, 11, 13, 29, 30, 31, 32, 44, 46, 47, 198, 209
Germany and Canada, 47
Ghai and Galli, 107
Ghana, 59
Ghandershe, 86
Great Depression, 29
Griffith, 10
Guled, iv, x

H

Hadith, 103, 217
Hamilton, 9
Harar, 86
Haud and Reserved Area, 87
Hawiye, 91, 92
Heavily Indebted Poor Countries Initiative, 116
Hersi, 123, 129, 130, 145, 146, 147, 158, 207
Herzegovina, 40, 42
Hiiraan, 112
Hirshabelle, xxviii, 99, 112, 129, 130, 131, 139, 140, 142, 144, 146, 147, 155, 179
Hirshabelle and Banadir, 139
His, xiii, xvii, xxi, 93, 98, 103
Hizbi Democratic Mustaqbal Somali, 94
Hobyo, 86
Horn of Africa, ix, x, xxviii, 85, 86, 87, 88, 97, 214
House, 195, 215
Hueglin, 18, 213

Hurricane Katrina, 22, 208

I

Ibn Battuta, 85, 208
Imbalances, 101
Impact of Civil War, 100
Independent Constitution Party, 97
Independent Constitutional Commission, 181
Independent Constitutional Review and Implementation Commission, 156
Independent Constitutional Review and Implementation Commission (ICRIC), 156
India, v, 10, 11, 32, 34, 35, 48, 52, 217, 218
Indian, 33, 216
Influences and Geopolitical Dynamics, 101
Innovations, 23
Intergovernmental Relations, 7, 113, 216
International Monetary Fund, 64, 116
Iraq, vi, 11, 40, 42, 43, 210, 212, 216
Iraqi, 41
Isaq, 91
Islam, vi, xix, 85, 102, 106, 215
Islamic, x, 90, 92, 98, 102, 103, 104, 105, 106
Islamic Union, 92, 98
Islamic Union Courts (IUC), 92
Islamist, 100
Italian, 88, 89, 94, 212, 219
Italian and British, 88

Italian Somaliland, 88, 94
Italian Somaliland and British Somaliland, 88
Italian Trusteeship, 89
Italians, 86, 87, 96
IUCs, 92, 98

J

Janeiro, 36
January, 92, 98
Jay and Madison, 9
Juba, 86
Jubaland, xxviii, 99, 127, 129, 130, 131, 133, 139, 140, 142, 144, 146, 147, 152, 154, 155, 179, 185
Jubaland and Puntland, 152, 185
July, 97
June, 97

K

Keil, 19, 21, 213
Kenya, xix, xxviii, 60, 87, 88, 89, 96, 97, 123
Khatumo, 174
KIIs, xxviii, xxix, 120, 123, 125, 137, 139, 140
KIIs and FGDs, xxix
KIIs. These, 120
Kurdistan, 41, 42
Kurds, 41

L

Labrador, 30
Land of Punt, 85
Länder, 10, 11, 30, 31
Lasqoray, 87

Latin, 5, 90, 211
Lausanne, 34
Legislative Assembly, 89
Light and Stieren, 10
Likert, 121, 137
London, 91, 211, 219
Lord, 103
Lower Juba, 127

M

Macedonia, 9
Majeerteen, 91
Major General Mohamed Siyad Barre, 90
Making Sense of Somali History, xix
Maxaa Tiri, 97
Mbagathi, 123, 128
Mbagathi Peace Process, 123
Menkhaus, 95, 215
Merca, 85, 87
Middle Belt, 74
Middle Juba, 127
Middle Shabelle, 112
Minister of Environment, xvii
Minister of Puntland, xxi
Ministry of Constitution, 166
Mirifle, 92, 97
Mississippi and New Mexico, 46
Mogadishu, iii, xxix, 85, 87, 109, 112, 117, 126, 127, 203
Mohamed Siyad Barre, 97
Mohiuddin and Islam, 103
Monetary, vii, 114
Mosley, 142, 215
Mudug, 112
Muslim, 85

Mutual Accountability Framework, 143, 182

N

National, vii, 11, 109, 114, 116, 125, 142, 148, 156, 159, 180, 182, 184, 185, 186, 210
National Capital District, 11
National Constituent Assembly, 109, 116
National Consultative Council, 142, 156, 159, 185
National Consultative Council (NCC), 156
National Leadership Forum, 125, 180, 184, 185
National Leadership Forum (NLF), 125, 180
Nepal, 11, 19, 210
Nevis Island, 12
New Brunswick, 47
New Deal, 29
New Guinea, 11
Newfoundland, 30
NFD, 88
NGOs, 24
Niger Delta, 37, 70, 73, 76
Nigeria, v, vi, 10, 11, 36, 37, 38, 39, 45, 47, 49, 52, 59, 60, 66, 67, 70, 71, 75, 177, 207, 211, 218
Nigeria and Brazil, 52
Nigeria and Cameroon, 59
Nigerian, 37, 39, 52, 57, 213
Nigerian Civil War, 57, 213
Nisa, 104
North and South Galkacyo, 132
Northern Frontier District (NFD), 87, 88
Northern Territory, 10

O

Ogaden, 87, 91, 96, 214
Omanis, 86
Oromia, 68, 72
Oromos, 70

P

Palmyra Atoll, 12
Pan, 97
Parliamentary Oversight Committee, 166
People, 133, 195, 209
PFC, 109, 110, 111, 112, 114, 115, 116, 117, 203, 217
PFC. This, 110
PhD, iii, xiii, xxiv, xxviii, 219
Political Will, 101
Portuguese, 87
President Abdurashid Ali Sharmarke of Somalia, 90
President and Vice President, 12
President of Puntland State of Somalia, xv, xvii
President Siyad Barre, 91
President Yeltsin, 37
Prime Minister of Somalia, xv
Prof. Abdurahman A. Baadiyow, xix
Professor Abdurahman A. Baadiyow, xiii
Professor Danial Ekongwe Awang, xiii
Professor Kenneth C. Wheare, 5
Professor Samuel Kale Ewusi, xiii
Prophet Muhammad, 103

Provisional Constitution, vii, 116, 217
Provisional Federal Constitution, xxviii, 108, 109, 110, 111, 115, 117, 175, 199, 201
Puerto Rico, 12
Puntland, xvii, xxi, xxiii, xxviii, 94, 99, 109, 113, 114, 115, 117, 121, 125, 128, 129, 130, 133, 139, 140, 142, 144, 146, 147, 154, 179
Puntland and Banadir, 140, 142, 144, 147
Puntland and Galmudug, 113, 129, 154
Puntland and Jubaland, 121
Puntland and Somaliland, 129
Puntland State, xvii, 109, 114, 117, 125, 128
Puntland State of Somalia, xvii
Putnam and Noor, 96

Q

Quebec, 30, 217
Queen Hatshepsut, 85

R

Rahanweyn Resistance Army (RRA), 92
Rahaweyn Resistance Army, 98
Region of Bougainville, 11
Republic of Somalia, xxix
Republika Srpska, 10, 40, 41
Resource Constraints, vii, 101
Respondents, 121, 137, 152, 165
Rome, 9, 92
Rothchild, 59, 60, 216, 217
Russia, v, 12, 36, 37, 38, 39, 218

Russian, 37, 38, 219
Rwanda, 17, 217
Rwandan Genocide, 57

S

Saddam Hussein, 41
Sahih Muslim, 103, 217
Said Barre, 178
Salah, iv, x, 103
Sanaag and Cayn, 174
São Paulo, 36, 47
São Paulo and Rio, 36
Sarajevo, 40
Schapiro, 20, 21, 218
Section, 142, 146
Security, 101, 107, 114, 211, 212
Security Force, 114
Serbian, 40
Shabaab, 92, 98, 100, 101
Shabelle, 86
Sharia, 102
Shiites, 41
Shura, 103, 215
SIDRA Institute, xxi
Siyad Barre, xvi, 92, 95, 98, 125, 130
Somali, vi, vii, ix, x, xvi, xvii, xix, xx, xxi, xxiii, xxiv, xxvii, xxxi, 72, 76, 84, 85, 86, 87, 88, 89, 90, 91, 92, 93, 94, 96, 97, 98, 99, 100, 101, 102, 103, 104, 105, 106, 108, 109, 116, 120, 123, 124, 125, 126, 128, 130, 131, 133, 142, 143, 144, 150, 151,152, 154, 155, 156, 157, 158, 159, 167, 169, 170, 171, 174, 176, 177, 178, 179, 180, 181, 182, 184, 185, 186, 189, 190, 193,

194, 195, 196, 197, 198, 199, 201, 202, 204, 205, 207, 209, 210, 211, 213, 214, 216, 218
Somali Democratic Movement (SDM), 92, 98
Somali Dialogue Platform, 143
Somali Federal Constitution, 116
Somali National League (SNL), 89
Somali National Movement, 91, 92, 98
Somali National Movement (SNM), 91, 92
Somali Patriotic Movement, 92, 98
Somali Patriotic Movement (SPM), 92
Somali Peninsula, 86
Somali Police Force, 97
Somali Provisional Constitution, 102
Somali Provisional Federal Constitution, 98
Somali Reconciliation Framework, 143
Somali Republic, 88, 97, 210
Somali Salvation Democratic Front, 92, 98
Somali Salvation Democratic Front (SSDF), 92
Somali Youth League (SYL), 88, 89
Somalia, iii, vi, vii, viii, ix, x, xv, xvi, xvii, xviii, xix, xx, xxi, xxiii, xxiv, xxv, xxvii, xxviii, xxix, xxx, xxxi, 12, 60, 72, 81, 84, 85, 86, 87, 88, 89, 90, 91, 92, 93, 95, 96, 97, 98, 99, 100, 101, 102, 103, 104, 105, 106, 108, 109, 110, 111, 113, 114, 115, 117, 120, 121, 122, 123, 124, 125, 126, 127, 128,
129, 130, 131, 132, 133, 134, 136, 137, 138, 139, 140, 141, 142, 143, 146, 148, 150, 151, 152, 155, 156, 157, 158, 162, 164, 165, 166, 167, 168, 169, 170, 171, 174, 175, 176, 177, 178, 179, 180, 181, 182, 184, 185, 187, 189, 190, 191, 192, 193, 194, 195, 196, 197, 199, 200, 201, 202, 203, 204, 205, 207, 209, 210, 211, 212, 214, 215, 216, 217
Somalia (AMISOM), 126
Somalia and Amhara, 72
Somalia National Army, 114, 171
Somalia National Front, 92, 98
Somalia National Front (SNF), 92
Somalia Provisional Federal Constitution, 117
Somalia Stability Fund, 143
Somaliland, xix, xxviii, 88, 91, 94, 114, 115, 129, 179, 208
Somalis, 70, 87, 88, 89, 96, 102, 125, 130, 132, 159, 198, 211, 217
Somalism, 97
Sonderbund War, 33
Soobe, 129
Sool, 174
South Africa, vi, 12, 60, 61, 62, 66, 68, 71, 74, 75, 140, 177, 197, 211, 218
South Africa and Rwanda, 140
South African, 140
South Sudan, 64
Southwest, xxviii, 99, 121, 128, 129, 130, 131, 139, 140, 142,

144, 146, 147, 152, 154, 155, 179
Southwest and Hirshabelle, 121
Sovereignty, 6, 215
Soviet, 37, 38, 39, 216, 218
Soviet Union, 37, 38, 39
Sparta, 9
St. Kitts and Nevis, 12
State, xvii, 109, 110, 113, 116, 117, 171, 209, 210, 211, 212, 214, 216, 218, 219
States of Micronesia, 11
Structure, 10, 11, 12, 170
Sudan, 12, 60, 177
Sudanese Civil Wars, 57
Suez Canal, 96
Sultanate, 86, 87
Sultanates, 86, 87
Sultanates and Kingdoms, 86
Sunnis, 41
Supreme Court, 31, 34, 39
Supreme Court of Canada, 31
Supreme Federal Court, 38
Supreme Revolutionary Council (SRC), 90
Swiss, 33, 49, 211, 215
Switzerland, v, 12, 32, 34, 35, 45
SYL, 89

T

Tanzania, 68
Territory and Population, 107
The Federalism Imperative, xxiv, xxv
The Federalist Papers, 9
The Qur, 103, 104
The Year of Africa, 58, 59
Tigray, 72

Tigrayans, 70
Togdheer and Sanaag, 113
Transitional Federal Charter, 108
Transitional Federal Government, xxviii, 98, 109
Tsarist, 37
Turks, 86

U

UN, 88
United Kingdom and Italy, 97
United Nations, 58, 63, 88, 219
United Nations Charter, 88
United Somali Congress, 92, 98
United Somali Congress (USC), 92
United States, v, 9, 12, 13, 22, 28, 29, 31, 32, 44, 45, 46, 47, 48, 51, 52, 53, 140, 197, 218
United States and Brazil, 47
United States and Germany, 28
United States of America, 9, 12
Upper House of Parliament, 156
US, 9, 22, 29, 31, 41, 44
US Supreme Court, 31

V

Verily, 104
Vladimir Putin, 37

W

Walloons, 70
Washington, 215
Watts, 13, 19, 64, 71, 219
Western, 62, 77, 78, 87, 210, 219
Western Cape, 62
Western Somali, 87

Westphalian, 14, 20, 21, 213, 218
World Bank, 64, 116, 208, 215
World War II, 10, 30

X

Xalay Dhaley, 204
Xeer, 102, 205, 216
Xisbiya, 129

Z

Zanzibarians, 86
Zayla, 85, 87
Zeila, 86

Milton Keynes UK
Ingram Content Group UK Ltd.
UKHW041304151124
2882UKWH00031B/112/J

9 781912 411832